Praise for *Living with Intent*

"Whether we know it or not, we matter; today matters. Mallika Chopra shows us all how to live quiet lives of inspiration. Her book and journey are not to be missed."

—Elizabeth Gilbert, bestselling author of *Eat, Pray, Love*

"More and more, people realize the value of approaching life with a mindful, purposeful spirit. With this insightful and often funny memoir, Mallika Chopra gives ideas and encouragement to anyone who wants to live with intent."

—Gretchen Rubin, bestselling author of
The Happiness Project and *Better Than Before*

"Clearly, Deepak is not the only lifestyle sage in the Chopra family. Mallika is warm, wise, and witty and *Living with Intent* is a wonderful and helpful read."

—Don Miguel Ruiz, bestselling author of *The Four Agreements*

"Mallika's unfettered account of her own path to intention gave me the comfort of knowing we all have our starts and stumbles in this arena, even a Chopra. She is an everywoman—an everymom—who openly struggles with life balance, spirituality, and insecurities like the rest of us. It's a twisty road, but her steps of INTENT help to gently bring things back into focus. I'm happy to be on my journey with my friend and fellow chocoholic Mallika."

—Jennifer Garner, actor

"How to live with intent?! To desire it is far from living it. Mallika Chopra leads the reader through her own path with bare honesty.... Parents who feel too busy with the minutiae of daily life will relate intimately to her experience.... [This] could start a global conversation about living with intent that we should all embrace."

—Elissa Epel, PhD, professor, UCSF Department of Psychiatry

"Mallika Chopra is a refreshingly honest writer who shares her transformative journey from stress, fear, doubt ... procrastination, and guilt into a life of true happiness and self-acceptance. This brilliant book provides a template of gentle, doable, baby-steps that will take you by the hand and lead you to living a joyful life. Reading this book is like having the world's best friend on speed dial."

—Arielle Ford, author of *The Soulmate Secret*

"When's the last time you slowed down, reflected deeply, and were satisfied with what you saw? In this warm, inspiring, and practical memoir, Mallika Chopra reconnects with her passions and daily purpose. For anyone interested in a journey of self-reflection and joyful discovery, Chopra makes a delightful companion and guide."

—Jack Canfield, coauthor of *Chicken Soup for the Soul* and *The Success Principles*

"*Living with Intent* offers us a gentle reminder that happiness and peace are a choice we make. This book awakens the presence of our inner wisdom and power so that we can enhance our capacity to serve the world."

—Gabrielle Bernstein, *New York Times* bestselling author of *Miracles Now*

"If you're spinning through your days wondering when you'll stop churning and instead start thriving, then you have to read Mallika's book. With humor, courage, and great insight she shares the keys to a purpose-filled life."
—Chade-Meng Tan, Jolly Good Fellow of Google and *New York Times* bestselling author of *Search Inside Yourself*

"Mallika Chopra has taught me through her powerful example of the importance of daily intentions. Through her personal story, Mallika sweetly reminds us of our own power to affect positive, lasting change in our lives, and consequently in the lives of everyone around us. Read this and prepare to have a big shift in perspective that changes everything for the positive."
—Tara Stiles, founder of Strala Yoga and author of *Make Your Own Rules Diet*

"Mallika Chopra's *Living with Intent* is a profoundly relatable roadmap for those of us struggling to stay afloat in our chaotic lives."
—Lisa Ling, journalist

"Throughout, her engaging voice offers relatable inspiration as though the two of you are chatting over tea—with intent."
—*LA Yoga*

"Mallika Chopra knows a thing or two about purpose. . . . In her new book, *Living with Intent*, she breaks down the differences between intents and goals and opens up about how becoming a mother helped her live a more purposeful life."
—*TIME*

LIVING

with

INTENT

HARMONY
BOOKS · NEW YORK

LIVING

with

INTENT

MY SOMEWHAT MESSY JOURNEY

TO PURPOSE, PEACE, AND JOY

MALLIKA CHOPRA

Afterword by Deepak Chopra

Harmony Books is a registered trademark, and the Circle
colophon is a trademark of Penguin Random House LLC.

Originally published in hardcover in the United States by Harmony Books,
an imprint of the Crown Publishing Group, a division of
Penguin Random House LLC, New York, in 2015.

Library of Congress Cataloging-in-Publication Data

Chopra, Mallika.
Living with intent : my somewhat messy journey to purpose,
peace, and joy / Mallika Chopra. — First edition.
pages cm
1. Self-realization—Religious aspects. 2. Intention. 3. Conduct
of life. 4. Spiritual life. 5. Chopra, Mallika. I. Title.
BL624.C47685 2015
204'.4—dc23
2014038008

ISBN 978-0-8041-3987-8
eBook ISBN 978-0-8041-3986-1

Printed in the United States of America

Book design by Meighan Cavanaugh
Illustrations by Yumi Sakugawa
Cover design by Jess Morphew
Cover art by Yumi Sakugawa

10 9 8 7 6 5 4 3 2 1

First Paperback Edition

For Sumant, Tara, and Leela,

From love comes purpose.

My love for you is overflowing,

unbounded, joyful.

CONTENTS

ACKNOWLEDGMENTS

It took me a long time to be ready emotionally to write this book.

It incubated for years. I'd write a proposal, edit, rewrite, throw it away, and start all over again from scratch. I gave up for months at a time, and then would go back to the proposal unclear yet again about what I was trying to say. But the intent to share my experiences was there, and with time the project took its own form.

The people along the way made it a reality and, ultimately, a joy to write.

To the angel investors of Intent, my deepest gratitude for believing in what we could create together. I thank you for your incredible generosity, patience, and belief that we can use social media to improve the world.

To my team at Intent, it has been a privilege to watch how you have realized your own intents, discovered purpose, and contributed to the world. Alex Bloomingdale, you have been as obstinate as I am in believing that we can create something meaningful with the Intent platform. Thank you for sharing my vision.

To the Intent community, those who have written for us, read and commented on our blogs, and shared your intents and supported others, you have brought life and passion to Intent, and, in turn, to my own personal journey.

To Carolyn Rangel, Felicia Rangel, Geeta Singh, and the team at the Chopra Center, your support, creative ideas, and outreach are appreciated more than I can express.

To Linda Loewenthal, my friend and literary agent, you so believed in this project that you put in hours of your time, editing and reworking the proposal. You were the champion who gave me the confidence that we could actually do this.

To Heather Jackson—we met as young mothers, sharing stories and promises inspired by love for our babies. What a joy to work together again on this book! Your notes are impeccable, and added such depth and structure to the book. Thank you also to Tina Constable for believing in the project, and to all the team members at Harmony who, I know, will add their own magic.

To Ginny Graves, this book is truly ours together. I no longer know where my words end and yours begin, as our journeys are so much the same. I loved our conversations over long, tasty lunches, brainstorming in that magical apartment in San Francisco, and e-mailing drafts and ideas back and forth between us. I know you put your heart and soul into this book, and for that I am forever grateful. I cannot wait to find another project to work on together.

To my friends who make up my village, together we have watched our children grow, shared fears and joys, celebrated births and mourned the deaths of some parents, admitted when we were overwhelmed and asked one another for help. Whether it's texting daily happenings, making quick phone calls to check in, catching up after the flag salute at school, celebrating our birthdays, chatting over lunch, going for walks, cleansing and exercising, brainstorming new business ideas, struggling with work-life balance, or liking Facebook status updates, our shared experiences have given me connection, comfort, happiness. You gave me ideas and inspiration through our conversations, our insecurities, our joys, and our resolutions to find balance and meaning. I am so incredibly grateful for all of you who have been there day in and day out for years now.

And to my family, I am blessed to have been born into a close-knit, loving one and to have married into another that has become my own. Mummy and Daddy, you have always believed in my talent and celebrated my work—I am incredibly grateful to have such incredible in-laws. Thank you to my father, who patiently brainstormed ideas, read every draft, and gave me honest feedback. I know this is a gift that many can't imagine. And to my mother, who remains my anchor for everything—truly everything—that I do. My gratitude to you is part of who I am. I aspire to be like you every day.

As I said in the dedication, love truly gives one purpose. I am awash with love, and for that I am truly grateful.

INTRODUCTION

It's 6:30 a.m., and I'm awakened by pop music. "I came in like a wrecking ball; I never hit so hard in love . . ."

Is that Miley Cyrus? I wonder blearily, as I reach to turn off my iPhone alarm. My überenthusiastic nine-year-old daughter, Leela, changes the song almost daily—which means I've been jarred from slumber by everyone from Lorde to Drake. Not what I would choose, but Leela's selections make me smile.

I jump out of bed to walk our dog, Yoda, while the girls get ready. We rush to school. I like to walk them in, but we're running late, so I just wave good-bye from the curb. The next few hours are a whirl of activity: meetings, errands, lunch on the go. There's never enough time, and I'm always feeling guilty about giving something short shrift. Either I don't make it to school for a class project or I skip a business meeting to help out at school; each makes me feel bad, so

I push myself to do as much as I can on both the work and parenting fronts. I survive by keeping my sugar and caffeine intake high—lots of tea, a double macchiato (or two) daily, and chocolate. I must have my chocolate.

As I sit in the carpool line, I dream about a blissful state of being well rested and energetic, eating healthy foods, exercising daily. I envision finally losing the extra ten pounds (OK, fifteen) that have hung around my waist for the last decade, and meditating so I can be more mindful in my activities. I imagine myself connecting with friends, having quiet dinners with my husband, and spending agenda-free time with my daughters, Tara and Leela. I also see myself volunteering in my community, feeling more connected to the larger world, and making a meaningful contribution. But that imagined reality is often shattered before the kids pile into the car and we rush to soccer practice. I sigh as I realize I forgot to pick up Yoda from the groomer and still need to get groceries before cooking dinner.

When I put the girls to bed, I'm exhausted. I catch up on e-mails, check social media, surf the Web for news, and, yes, peek at celebrity gossip sites. More often than I like to admit, I crawl into bed wondering what I did all day.

Am I nurturing my body, my mind, my soul?

I think about what's going on in the world and wish I could do more to give back.

What is my purpose? How can I serve? Am I living with intent?

Asking such questions has been a part of my life even if I have not always lived the answers to their fullest potential. When we were young, my father encouraged my brother and me to start every day by consciously thinking about what we wanted. We had a tradition in our house after meditation: my father would ask us to say the following phrase from *A Course in Miracles*:

I am responsible for what I see
I choose the feelings I experience
And set the goals I will achieve.
And everything that seems to happen to me
I ask for, and receive as I have asked.

Then he would ask us the question that still echoes in my mind:

What do you want?

Being kids, our responses included things like a new computer game, tickets to the Celtics, and a trip to Hawaii. My father would listen patiently and acknowledge our material desires and then he would gently ask:

"How about love? Compassion? Connection? Inspiration? Purpose?"

We were taught at a very young age to ask daily for the qualities in our lives that would make us feel happy, loved, secure, energized, and purposeful. And through this process we began each day setting an intention, a desire or dream that we wanted to pursue, and actively seeking the emotional and spiritual connections to make it happen.

Now, many decades later, I feel an urgent need to get back to that practice. Starting Intent.com was a first step. The website gives me and other members a place to share our aspirations, receive support, and, ultimately, transform our dreams into reality. Over the years, I've discovered that when you ask people what they want, what they *truly* want, they usually answer with some variation of these themes: love, connection, health, purpose, inspiration, and significance.

It's reassuring to realize I'm not alone in questioning whether there is a less bumpy path to more joy and purpose in my life. As I listen to those in my community—fellow moms and dads, work colleagues, members of Intent.com, or people who attend my speeches—I hear that many are stretched too thin. Whether single, married, looking for work, working parents or stay-at-home moms or dads, people are often doing too many things, feeling guilty or inadequate about what they're not doing, and desperately hoping for a renewed sense of purpose. They are also often not making time to nurture themselves as they pursue ambitions and care for others. And they, like me, are passing on the same nonstop-doing mode to their children.

I do believe there is hope for all of us to live a life that is more meaningful, inspiring, and fun. By identifying our intentions—the seeds of our deepest longings—stating them and ultimately pursuing them, we're more likely to find the path to happiness, meaning, and relevance in our world. Intents help us create the lives we want to live. Moreover, when we consciously set an intent, we put in motion a process to make it happen. We become more aware of people who can help us, and we take advantage of encounters and opportunities. We notice coincidences and attract teachers, allies, and guides. We start behaving *as if* what we want will really happen, and often it actually occurs.

This book is a chronicle of my intention and search to find more meaning, more joy, and more balance in my life. My hope is that by telling my story, I can share some of the wisdom I have gathered from friends, experts, and family as well as inspire others with my own successes (and failures). Along the way, I provide a practical road map for how we all can move from thought to action to outcome—and realize our intentions. I devote a chapter to each step on my journey and each piece of my INTENT action plan: Incubate, Notice, Trust, Express, Nurture, and Take Action.

As you read this book, I hope you will be motivated by the changes I make and are inspired by others' stories, intrigued by some of the fascinating scientific findings, and encouraged and supported by the insights you come across along the way. I also hope you will share your intents and experiences on Intent.com or our Intent app.

Beyond all else, my heartfelt intention is for this book to spark a global conversation about living with intent, one that provides hope to those who feel dissatisfied, encourages those who are eager to discover their own passions, and gives us all the opportunity to support one another in our quest for balance and purpose, connection, and joy.

LIVING

with

INTENT

ONE

THE PATH TO INTENT

I'm speaking at a health and wellness conference when I'm struck by a disconcerting thought: *Who are you to be talking about intention when you're not living yours?* About fifty people are in the audience, mostly women thirty-five and older, and they're listening keenly as I explain concepts about health, balance, and living a life of purpose.

"Intents are expressions of who we aspire to be as individuals—physically, emotionally, spiritually—as members of our families and communities, and even as citizens of Mother Earth. Intents are a way of defining what we want and asking the universe or God for help. They're the seeds of what we yearn for in our lives,

> "Intents are expressions of who we aspire to be as individuals—physically, emotionally, spiritually—as members of our families and communities, and even as citizens of Mother Earth."

whether it is better health, meaningful relationships, or love."

I can see people nodding their heads and jotting down notes.

Well, at least they're engaged.

"In fact," I continue, "a seed is an extraordinarily apt metaphor. A seed already contains the essence of what it can eventually become; but in order for it to thrive, you have to plant it, water it, nurture it. You consciously focus on the idea and take action to make it happen. Like a seed, an intent is a morsel of possibility bursting with surprising potential."

The seed is a powerful metaphor for intent. A seed is often planted deep in the ground, beginning its life in darkness—the same place our intents initially take root: in the shadowy depths within our minds where dissatisfaction, sadness, fear, but also joy, hope, and motivation dwell. The darkness provides surprisingly fertile ground for the seed of intent to grow, giving us the motivation and inspiration to make an effort to change.

I continue to explain the concept and mention my father, which of course has everyone nodding with enthusiastic approval. "My father taught us that intent has within it the mechanisms for its own fulfillment, as a seed has within it everything it needs to become a tree, a flower, a piece of fruit. Intent is a seed in consciousness, or spirit, and you have the power to bring it into reality."

I say the words, and yet, at that particular moment, I feel strangely alienated from these concepts I hold so dear to my heart. Prior to the talk, my day was chaotic. I'd been running late on my way to the event and spilled coffee on my pants. The giant chocolate chip cookie I'd eaten an hour or so before had left me with a queasy sugar hangover. And earlier that day, I'd missed an important phone call for work, a lapse that left me feeling guilty and shaken. I am particular, in general, about being on time and being dependable in my commitments. When I am not, I am not so self-forgiving. But it's not just today that's the problem; on a broader level, I don't feel as if I'm living with intent. Instead of living consciously, I'm often overwhelmed and scrambling to catch up. As I stand on stage, sharing my ideas, I feel like a bit of a fraud. I believe the words I'm saying, deeply and wholeheartedly, but I'm not putting them into action. I'm not living them.

Needing an escape from these thoughts, I ask my audience to close their eyes while I guide them in a meditation. After five minutes of deep breathing and silence, I tell them to listen to my questions.

"There is no need to answer these questions, just experience them," I say.

"Who am I?
"What do I want?
"How can I serve?"

This meditation is as much for me as my audience. I need to get centered, to get in touch with the core of who I am. I take a few deep breaths. And I feel those questions in every cell. *Who am I? What do I want? How can I serve?* I've thought about them so many times. For much of my childhood, it was a family ritual for my dad to ask us those questions. But now, on stage, I feel them in a different way. My awareness is anchored in the present, in my body, mind, and spirit, and I feel open and receptive. Some answers bubble immediately to the surface:

> "Who am I?
> "What do I want?
> "How can I serve?"

WHO AM I?

A mother of two wonderful daughters: a wife, a daughter, a sister, a friend.

An entrepreneur, an author.

A soccer mom, a role I wear grudgingly; like a too-tight shirt, it chafes and binds, though why I'm not sure.

A soul who loves and wants to feel loved.

WHAT DO I WANT?

Health for my family and for me.

Financial security.

Love, purpose. *But how do I get it?*
Peace, rest, balance. *None of which seems doable at the moment.*

HOW CAN I SERVE?
Right now, as a mom. Beyond that, I don't really
  know.
Is that enough?
Is there more that will give me a deeper sense of
  purpose?

As I continue to guide the audience through the meditation, my own answers—and the questions they raise—echo in my mind. As I ask the audience to reflect on who they are, I realize I've in some fundamental way lost the innate sense of who I am—or at least the sense of where I fit in, and what I'm supposed to be doing with my life. I have lost an important connection to my soul.

The revelation makes me acutely uncomfortable, and I have to fight the urge to let my mind wander away from that insight. But the more I sit with those thoughts, distressing as they are, the more I learn. I listen to my body and have to admit that I'm not in optimal health. I feel overweight, tired, and achy. Despite my family's focus on spirituality, I am not living a life filled with meditation, yoga, cleanses, spiritual retreats, and vegan meals. In fact, my addiction to sugar drives me to increasingly unhealthy behavior. Too often I make surreptitious outings in the middle of the day to buy cookies or cupcakes, and then devour them without telling anyone. I'm not taking care of myself in other ways either. I exercise infrequently and stay up far too late reading posts on Facebook or playing video games. I always have an excuse for skimping on the essentials of good health, but I know my excuses are flimsy and merely a cover for my own unwillingness to take the steps that are required to make difficult changes. My daughter Leela has inherited my love of sugar and is developing similarly unhealthy eating habits. As I stand there thinking this, I understand that her behavior is a mirror of my own. With that realization, I'm beset by the nearly universal emotion of motherhood: guilt.

As I lead the group to the final of my father's questions, I find that, if possible, I'm even more overwhelmed and confused. *How can I serve?* I know I want to do something more, but honestly, I have no idea what that "something" is—and I am too tired to think about it or put much energy toward it. After years of spinning on the merry-go-round of family and work, I'm dizzy and disoriented. And I want to get off.

So is and does everyone else, I tell myself. I'm not alone. I let my mind wander, thinking about ways in which I'd feel more satisfied. I recall the period when I was writing my first two books, when the girls were younger. Those projects helped me formulate my thoughts about parenthood and find my way as a mother. Could writing a book, about intent, help guide my path and help me find my way forward?

The more I think about it, the more sense it makes. So in that moment, in front of a crowd of people meditating, I silently set the intent to write this book—and to seek guidance from those who inspire me and share my quest.

The concept of intent has been a part of my family story for as long as I can remember. Our champion of intent was Maa, my grandmother. She held an unshakable belief in the power of wishes, prayer, and magic. Maa was even convinced that the color of her sari would influence the national cricket match. Red was her color of preference for home matches. Maa also had faith that prayer could help my grandfather's patients get well. She would visit them in the hospital, and then go to the temple with specific offerings to benefit their healing. Maa knew that her thoughts and desires shaped the world, and indeed she had a remarkable ability to create her own reality. One example has become family lore, and as a child, as I learned about intention, this story bolstered my faith in its power.

In 1954, several years after India gained independence from the British Empire, my grandparents and my father and his younger brother lived in Lucknow, where my grandfather, an army doctor, was stationed. The first-ever prime minister of India, Jawaharlal Nehru, was visiting the city as part of the celebration for this new nation. Like everyone in the village, Maa was abuzz with anticipation and spent weeks thinking about which sari she would wear, how to fix her hair, whether she should wear flat shoes or heels. My grandfather, dad, and uncle teased her about her obsession and warned her not to get her hopes up; in that crush of people there was simply no way the prime minister would notice one woman's sari, they told her. Maa let them laugh, but she remained undeterred.

"Not only will Nehru notice me," she assured them, "he'll personally give me his blessing."

The day finally arrived and my grandfather, father, and uncle ventured out onto the street at four a.m. to secure the family's spot for the parade. Maa, wearing an eye-catching brilliant pink sari, joined them later that morning. By the time the motorcade began, the streets were a mass of humanity as thousands of people eagerly awaited Nehru's arrival. As the motorcade slowly approached the spot where Maa and her family stood, Nehru waved from the open window of his limousine. In the middle of the screaming crowds, my grandmother stood silently, her palms together in front of her heart in the traditional Namaste greeting.

And as if she willed it, Nehru's car stopped. The prime minister got out and walked through the crowd to where my grandmother stood. He put his hands together in a sign of respect, removed the rose from his lapel, and, as the throng watched, handed the rose to Maa. He then returned to his car and departed. While the crowds around her cheered, Maa's eyes sparkled, and she looked at my grandfather and winked.

With Maa's spirit guiding me, I plunge into my research on intent. The stack of books on my bedside table, then on the floor next to it, grows by the day. I pick up books by authors I've long heard about—some of whom I've known since I was a child—but have never read. My dad for one. Eckhart Tolle. Marianne Williamson. Arianna Huffington. Andrew Weil. Dan Siegel. I set the intent to speak to these incredible teachers and learn from them. I spend an afternoon drafting e-mails to them, and decide that if it is meant to happen, they will agree to be interviewed.

Meanwhile, I turn the concept of intent over and over in my mind. Examining it from all angles, I realize even the word is a little fuzzy and ill defined. What do we mean when we talk about intention?

Intents aren't merely goals. They come from the soul, from somewhere deep inside us where we get clarity on our heartfelt desires for happiness, acceptance, health, and love. By thinking about our intents, cultivating and expressing them, we create the climate in which they're more likely to happen. But intents also need to be nurtured, to be given time to come to fruition. And at the right time in our lives we need to take action and make an effort to encourage and foster their fulfillment.

The notion of intent goes back millennia. Wisdom traditions from around the world talk about intent as the driving force of creation, and the concept plays a significant role in a number of religious creeds, including Hinduism and Buddhism. Intention in Sanskrit is *Samkalpa*, or an idea formed in the mind or heart. "Right intention" is the second element of the Buddha's Noble Eightfold Path, the teachings that describe the way to end personal suffering and achieve enlightenment. Right intention says essentially: treat yourself and others with kindness and compassion while living in alignment with your deepest values.

In the Buddhist tradition, intention is about living each moment with integrity and in keeping with what matters most to you. Buddhists believe that by carrying your intentions with you moment to moment and trying to live in accord with your deepest values, you are more likely to set wise goals—and do the necessary work to achieve them.

The Hebrew word *kavanah* describes the total awareness and attention you should strive to bring to every moment of your life; it's a way of giving meaning to your actions. For instance, prayer without *kavanah*, or intention, is little more than meaningless words. Even Christian prayer in which you ask God for what you want can be thought of as a form of intention.

More recently, scientists have tried to sort out how—or if—intent works, and most of the research has focused on intercessory prayer. Can praying for people help them heal? The results are mixed. Some studies show a robust effect, some none at all. But in one recent study investigators at Royal Adelaide Hospital Cancer Centre in Australia looked at whether prayer could improve cancer patients' spiritual and emotional well-being. For six months, a Christian prayer group from a church some distance away prayed for slightly more than half the patients. When compared with the control group, who didn't receive the church's prayers, the prayed-for patients showed small but significant improvements in spiritual and emotional well-being. They had no idea that they were being prayed for, but they improved anyway.

By what mechanism could prayer heal these patients? My father believes that consciousness itself is a fundamental force—as basic as gravity—but one we don't yet have the scientific tools to understand. It could be that conscious intention generates electrostatic or magnetic energy, and the invisible flow has a small but measurable effect on behavior—our own as well as others'. In any case, there's solid evidence for one piece of the puzzle: our thoughts and beliefs can affect our own health.

Just look at the placebo effect, in which a sham treatment produces positive results merely because the patient believes it will. Placebos work almost as well as potent antidepressants in treating mild to moderate depression, and they've been shown to reduce symptoms in Parkinson's, Crohn's disease, and multiple sclerosis. Our minds have a powerful influence on our bodies—and our lives. So why not use our minds to improve our lives? Why not set an intention to become a more caring person, to attract love, or to contribute to the betterment of humanity?

> Embracing small personal changes can be the first step toward creating greater change in the world, and humanity at large.

What would you like to change? What parts of your life aren't working? What's missing? By considering these questions, you can uncover the seeds of your deepest longings. What small changes can you make to feel more rested, happier, more connected, more inspired? Embracing small personal changes can be the first step toward creating greater change in the world, and humanity at large.

To my delight, I receive a response to one of my e-mails from a consultant to Eckhart Tolle TV. He tells me that Tolle will be in San Francisco for a speech, and while he won't be taking private meetings, he has agreed to meet me because he is intrigued and excited by the concept of intent. When the day arrives, I'm nervous. He's revered for his work in the realm of spirituality and transforming consciousness, and my father has told me he truly lives in the present moment and is connected to spirit at a deep level. I don't want to look like a total flake.

To make things worse, I'm beset by the worst allergies I've had in years. I sneeze for three hours straight before our meeting, worrying the whole time about whether I should go through with the interview. My eyes are red and runny, my nose dripping, my throat cracking and swollen. I pick up the phone several times to call and cancel, then set it back down. I don't want to miss the opportunity to talk to Tolle, so I take a deep breath and forge ahead. And when we sit down together, the sneezing stops.

As I ask Tolle my main questions—*What is intention? How do you define it and bring intentions to life?*—some church bells ring in the distance. Attuned to the present, as my father had promised, Tolle lights up and says the chimes take him back to his younger days in Europe. We spend a moment just listening, and something about the lovely sound, combined with his calm, welcoming presence, soothes me and puts me at ease.

"At its most basic, intention is a thought that arises in the mind and wants to manifest in the external world. On a cosmic scale, before something manifests, it is probably already there in the mind of God," he says.

"In order to identify an intent, instead of asking yourself *What do I want?* a better question might be: *What does the universe want from me?* or *What can I give the universe?* It's easy to get caught up in desires that are driven by your ego, but asking those questions can help you focus on a purpose that is greater than yourself. That doesn't mean the purpose has to be something world changing.

"Many people believe that following their purpose means doing something grand. The truth is, greatness may be hidden in the everyday activities of work and parenting. If you think of intention as a desire that wants to manifest through you, you can become a vehicle for achieving ambitions that go beyond your own ego."

> "The truth is, greatness may be hidden in the everyday activities of work and parenting."

His comments remind me that intents don't come from the mind, but rather from the soul. They need to be guided by deeper, more selfless motives. And when they are, wonderful things can happen. Tolle tells me about the years he spent in England, doing "small-scale" spiritual teachings. Maybe ten people would turn up at his workshops, and sometimes there was just one.

"I taught anyway," he says. "I felt that was my life's purpose."

Then after a few years he sensed something stirring within him.

"It wasn't dissatisfaction but this feeling that there was something bigger I needed to do that hadn't expressed itself yet. Something wanted to be born, and I had to enable it to come out into the world."

Around this time, he visited a country church in the village of Somerset, and without thinking about it he spoke the words "I'd like acceleration, please." A few weeks later he woke up knowing he needed to move to the northeast coast of the United States to write a book.

"Something wanted to be created, and I felt it was a book," he says. "It didn't feel like my idea. If you're open to what the universe wants done in this world, conscious doing happens through you."

I tell Tolle that while being a mom is the most important thing in my life, I sometimes worry that it isn't enough. He smiles, almost like my grandfather would when I needed reassurance.

"There are people who are happy to be doing small things," he says. "I call them frequency holders. They are just as important as those who create big things. Their purpose is to give their full attention to the present moment and to every action and interaction with other human beings—to be fully aware even in the smallest interactions. In that way, they also change the world for the better. In our culture, frequency holders aren't often recognized, but that doesn't mean they're not important. I was a frequency holder for a long time and still am in many ways."

I leave the interview feeling a little dazed but also moved and inspired. I contemplate what it means to be what he calls a frequency holder. In a way, it sounds a lot like being a soccer mom. Is it my ego saying I need to do something more, or is there truly something greater I need to create? If I am a frequency holder, how can I happily embrace that role and become more anchored in the present and more able to bring my best self to my family and friends? How can I stop feeling so guilty, overwhelmed, and insufficient?

As I head to the airport, I start thinking about my to-do list and realize I still have to order the blueberry muffins for the class party. I start sneezing again, and my eyes begin to itch. It hits me that while I sat with Eckhart, I didn't sneeze at all. I was feeling truly peaceful and in the present moment. I had been told by his associate that we would have fifteen minutes to chat, but we spoke for more than an hour. I feel immense gratitude.

And as I make my way through the crowded security line, I do something I've never done before: head to the bar and order a double Macallan scotch whiskey. It settles the sneezing and my racing thoughts. I'm sure this isn't what Tolle had in mind, but in this moment—and this moment is all I really have, as he would remind me—it works.

Not long after my interview with Tolle, I'm sitting at home one day mulling the idea of intent. While I fully believe that intention is a powerful tool for personal change, I also know from those in our community and my own experience that putting the concept into practice can feel confusing. Is there a way to describe the process that would make it clearer and simpler? As I'm trying to sort out the issue, my practical, analytical left brain kicks into gear.

For the next few days, I keep a pen and paper handy, and every time I come up with a word that helps define intent or seems to be an important part of the intent process, I jot it down. I wind up with about twenty words and ideas, from "meditate" to "network with friends" to "pay attention to coincidences." A fan of acronyms, I start playing with some of the core concepts to see if I can come up with a sort of road map for fulfilling intents. Eventually I hit upon six strategies that can help us all find our way forward, INTENT: Incubate, Notice, Trust, Express, Nurture, and Take Action.

Incubate:
Quiet your mind to tap into your deepest intentions; see where this leads.

Notice:
Become mindful of your thoughts and actions and pay attention to what they tell you about what gives you meaning and a sense of purpose—and look for signs that can point you toward your true path.

Trust:
Have confidence in your inner knowing—and in the messages the universe sends you—and allow that knowledge to guide you forward.

Express:
Write down your intentions, say them out loud or share them with others to fully embrace them and help you move ahead in your journey.

Nurture:
Be gentle with yourself as you try to find your way. Intention isn't always a straightforward path, just as life isn't. Giving

yourself opportunities to try—and fail—is often part of, and even crucial to, the process.

Take Action:
Once you've identified an intent, or even multiple ones, don't sit and wait for it to magically manifest; instead take the practical steps that can make each become a reality. It may be easiest to choose one intent first, and set short-term goals to help you get started.

Why take the trouble to try to live with intention? Why not just drift along without making the effort to clarify what you want? Years ago, David Sable, the CEO of Young & Rubicam (now Y&R), told me this Hasidic tale that gets at the heart of why I believe so deeply in making an effort to live with intent:

> *The great Rabbi Zusya was lying on his deathbed, tears streaming down his face. When his followers asked him why he was crying, he said, "If God asks me why I wasn't like Moses, I'll say I wasn't blessed with that kind of leadership ability or wisdom. But if God asks me, 'Zusya, why weren't you Zusya? Why didn't you fulfill your own highest potential? Why didn't you find your inner self?' What will I say then?"*

I want to live my life to its fullest potential. I want to embrace my own purpose, however large or small it may be. I want to find my own Nehru moments and take positive steps toward becoming the person I am meant to be. The journey will undoubtedly be a winding one, filled with surprises and setbacks as well as gifts. But I'm ready to embrace it fully, wherever it may take me.

Where would you like to go? What's calling to you? Let's start that journey together.

INTENTIONAL LIVING:
REFLECTIONS AND PRACTICES

Below are some things that have helped me as I clear the obstacles from my path. I share them in the hopes that they might inspire and help you as well:

1. Go for a walk outside. Notice and appreciate how intention plays itself out in the universe—how a flock of birds turns at the same time or how an army of ants marches to its own rhythm. It is powerful just to notice and appreciate what's around you, without feeling pressure to do anything more. For some, writing down free-flowing thoughts or observations in a journal is a great exercise for continued quiet reflection.

2. Plant a seed in your garden or in a pot on a sunny windowsill in your home. It can be any type of seed—flower, fruit, or vegetable. Take responsibility for watering it daily and exposing it to sunlight. Enjoy its beauty and your nurturing power when the seed blossoms into its own unique expression.

3. Identify a person in your family or your community who is what Eckart Tolle would call a

frequency holder. It may be anyone—your mom, the postman, or the clerk at the grocery store—someone who you feel appears to be living daily with intention. Appreciate the important role that person plays in the lives around her or him.

INTENT PRACTICE: "WHAT DOES THE UNIVERSE WANT FROM ME?"

- Set aside five minutes to meditate or just sit quietly. Choose a place where you feel happy and secure.
- Take a few minutes to settle down, breathing in deeply, inhaling and exhaling comfortably. Not trying to control your breath, not trying to control anything. Just letting it flow and its rhythm relax you.
- Ask yourself the following questions. Don't feel the need to answer the questions. Just take time to experience what comes up when you ask.

Who am I?
Pause for a few seconds, and repeat the question.

What do I want?
Pause again for a few seconds, and then repeat the question.

How can I serve?
Pause, then repeat the question.

- Take another deep breath and ask yourself:

What does the universe (God, or whatever spiritual presence you believe in) want from me?
Again, do not feel as if you need to have a clear answer to these questions. Just see what percolates in these quiet moments.

TWO

INCUBATE

I awaken early on July 24 to the sound of singing. *Happy birthday to you, happy birthday to you, happy birthday dear Mommy, happy birthday to you.* Sumant and the girls serenade me, and as I sit up in bed, they place a breakfast tray in front of me. Tara and Leela are beaming, clearly proud of their accomplishment. A chocolate croissant, strawberries, my macchiato, and handmade gifts and cards. The perfect way to start my forty-second year: filled with love and pastries.

Not long after delivering my breakfast and birthday hugs, they leave to give me some time alone this morning—my one request for the day. I've set aside this time to begin meditating. Again. I've gone through phases of being diligent about the practice, but for the past few years I've let it lapse. My birthday, at the beginning of my journey toward living with intention, seems like a perfect day to recommit.

The best part of committing to a daily practice: I'll cultivate more mindfulness—an awareness of what's happening in the present moment, externally and internally—which will help me understand why I feel so drained and help me discover what will fill me up. This is part of the incubation phase for me—finding stillness and silence so I can pay attention to what my body and mind are asking of me.

I clear a space in the corner of our bedroom and move one of my favorite comfy chairs into the nook. I place a small Buddha I've had for years on the floor in front of the chair, then prop two photos against it. One was taken during a family visit to the Taj Mahal. The girls are smiling; Sumant and I look happy and relaxed. The other shows me and Sumant at our wedding ceremony. We're sitting on the dais, our family around us. My paternal grandfather, whom I called Daddy, sits in the foreground. He passed away long ago, but I feel his comforting presence still—and this image reminds me he's here in spirit, supporting me as always. I feel loved and confident when I remember my grandfather, realizing that all those special moments we spent together when I was young will be with me forever. The photos make me feel these things—just the emotions I need to guide me into the future. I sit in my chair (the lotus position on the floor is too uncomfortable for me, and I don't want to be distracted by pain) and close my eyes.

Meditation has been a meaningful part of my life for a long time, providing me the opportunity to settle my mind, slough off stress, center my emotions, and connect with the quieter voice within. If I truly want to define and pursue my intents, I can't possibly do it without this contemplative practice.

I've found that sitting in silence and focusing the mind is the most meaningful and effective way to incubate intents, because it provides access to a deeper well of understanding, insight, and awareness. To tap into your intents, you need to know yourself; meditation helps reveal your thought processes, your fears, your insecurities, your strengths, and your passions. Once you're aware of those aspects of yourself, you're better able to identify the thoughts and beliefs that are holding you back and home in on the activities, people, and practices that lift you up. In other words, you're ready and more able to live with intent.

> To tap into your intents, you need to know yourself; meditation helps reveal your thought processes, your fears, your insecurities, your strengths, and your passions.

Meditation isn't the only way to incubate your intentions. But cultivating a quiet, contemplative mind-set is key to this step. I also have important insights when I run on the beach or take a walk in the woods or do yoga—or sometimes even when I'm sitting and doing a puzzle. We all have our own ways of finding contemplative time and space. Maybe for you it is baking, knitting, dancing, or sitting and listening to music. Meditating is the quickest, most effective way for me to connect to that place where my mind is calm, but there's no one right avenue. Incubating can happen anytime you give yourself the gift of time to reflect and relax, to honor stillness and silence.

Over the years, I've learned that by quieting my mind I can leave behind the physical and emotional distractions of daily life and connect with who I really am, beyond the external labels and internal dialogue that runs like a noisy ticker tape in my brain. Once I've reached that silent place, I can hear the softer voice of my true self—the one that knows what will make me feel happy, connected, purposeful, and content.

"Before anybody can even think about their intentions and what they want out of life, they need to discover what it means to be present."

Meditation is also the most effective way to anchor myself in the here and now. As Eckhart Tolle told me during our conversation: "Before anybody can even think about their intentions and what they want out of life, they need to discover what it means to be present." The present is where the key to my happiness lies, because it's really all I—or any of us—have.

It's not necessary to make a special meditation altar. I could just sit on my bed or my bedroom floor and close my eyes. But creating a ritual around meditation helps me get in the mood and shifts my mind toward contemplation and introspection. As I sit down in my special chair, legs planted comfortably on the floor and hands in my lap, I inhale deeply and let my breath out in a long, slow exhale, then do it again. I'm trying to shake off my doing mode and shift into sitting mode—and suddenly I'm overwhelmed by emotion. My chest is tight, my throat constricts, and I feel the familiar salty sting of tears in my eyes. It's not sadness that moves me, but gratitude. Gratitude to Sumant, Tara, and Leela for giving me this opportunity to sit and breathe. Gratitude to the publishers of my book, who have encouraged (and paid) me to go on this journey of self-discovery. And gratitude for the practice of meditation itself.

Sitting here preparing to quiet my mind feels like coming home—to my family and my childhood. This practice has meant the world to us. The truth is, my entire life changed—our family's life changed—when my father discovered meditation.

Despite growing up in India, my parents did not have much experience when they were young with meditation and Ayurveda—things my father is now well known for advocating. They were raised with more Western values. All four of my grandparents were well educated, and following marriage, both sets lived in England for a time after India was liberated from British rule in 1947. As a result, both my parents learned to speak impeccable English. To this day, my dad can recite every Shakespeare play from beginning to end. My father studied Western medicine—the option "smart" Indians pursued at the time, if they didn't become engineers—and after he finished medical school, my newly married parents immigrated to the United States in 1970 for his residency.

By the time they had been in the country a decade, my father was a successful physician. I was nine, and my brother, Gotham, was five. We were well-adjusted American kids with strong ties to our family, our Indian community, and our American school. But we weren't a particularly spiritual family. We celebrated Diwali, the major Hindu festival in the fall, and Holi, the festival of colors that celebrates the coming of spring by throwing colored powder and water all over ourselves and the other celebrants.

From my child's perspective, we were happy. What I didn't realize then was how much my father was suffering under the stress of his career. He felt as if he were on autopilot, pushing pills to his patients. He smoked incessantly, and my parents argued frequently about his drinking. One terrifying morning their tension came to a head, and my mother packed a bag. I remember feeling confused. *Where is she going?* I wondered. They screamed at each other as she headed toward the door. My mom got in her car to drive away, but Gotham ran to the driveway and lay down behind the rear wheels. It suddenly clicked for me. She was leaving.

For the first time ever, I felt truly afraid. I'd always taken our safety and happiness for granted. What was happening to our family?

The confrontation served as one of several wake-up calls for my father. He was unhappy and went looking for solutions. Long a student of philosophy, he attended a talk by Jiddu Krishnamurti, an Indian philosopher and writer who explored consciousness and the nature of human existence. After hearing the speech, my father began poring over Krishnamurti's books and audio recordings. Through him, he learned about meditation, a practice that Krishnamurti called extraordinary. "If you do not know what it is like you are like the blind man in a world of bright color, shadows and moving light," he wrote. Intrigued, my father signed up for a course at the Transcendental Meditation Center in Cambridge.

We've heard the story of his first experience at the Center many times. When he meditated that day, he says, he felt a sense of peace and silence that was missing from his life. He felt a connection to himself, and to a larger spirit, and the effect was so powerful it changed everything. As was typical for my dad, he wanted to share and explore this incredible experience with others. He rushed home, picked up my mother, and took her straight back to the TM Center so she could experience for herself what he'd discovered. For my quiet, calm mom, the silence and stillness of meditation felt natural, and she took to it quickly, developing a committed practice from that day on. Thanks to my father's enthusiasm, it didn't take long before our whole Indian community was meditating.

From then on, life in our house was different. My father quit smoking and drinking. Our family spent more time together. The undercurrent of tension eased. When I came home from school, I'd do homework, watch a little TV, then spend fifteen minutes meditating with my mom before dinner. I learned to love the feeling of quieting my mind and connecting with the present moment. Sitting there with my mother made me feel safe—and because I'd had a glimpse of what unsafe could feel like, those shared meditations felt like a lifeline, tethering our family together.

Learning to meditate inspired my father to dive into the burgeoning new field of mind/body medicine, launching him on an unexpected and stunning journey to worldwide renown. So I saw firsthand the power this simple practice has to transform people's lives.

Now, as I sit in my own home in front of my newly created altar and close my eyes, I feel I'm reconnecting not only with a family legacy but also with a source of potential—the potential for my *own* transformation. I focus my mind on my breath, feeling the cool air moving in through my nostrils and down to my belly, then experience the sensation as it leaves my body. I marvel, as always, that this life-giving function of breathing takes place constantly without my conscious control, or even awareness. But when I focus on it, it is there, steady and reliable. Then, as I inhale, I mentally say my mantra, Sanskrit for "tool of the mind." A mantra is a sound or word that is used in meditation, chanting, or prayer. Most mantras are soothing—many people use the word "love" or "peace"—and give the mind something to focus on to help break the constant cycle of thoughts. I was given my mantra by a teacher at the Chopra Center more than twenty years ago when I began practicing Primordial Sound Meditation (a form of meditation that I now teach). My mantra is based on the vibrational energy of the universe when I was born. It is one of hundreds used in the Vedic tradition that dates back thousands of years. It's difficult to describe what it sounds like. Think of primordial sounds—waves lapping against the shore or a breeze blowing through the trees. They're sounds that heal. That's what my mantra feels like.

I mentally repeat this sound now and it resonates in my heart. I continue to repeat it, and when my mind drifts away into thinking, as it always does, I gently return my attention to my mantra. I could just focus on my breath, on the gentle in-and-out sensation of air moving through my nostrils, but because I've been using a mantra since childhood, the sound helps me settle down, cueing my mind that it's time to shift from thinking to being mode. It's like walking down a well-worn path that leads to a familiar place of stillness.

Several breaths later, I realize I'm thinking about Tara's choices for middle school next year, what snacks to get for Leela's soccer game, writing an update for my investors of Intent—the familiar mix of worry, anticipation, and dread carrying me away from the present moment. I acknowledge these thoughts without judging them—thinking is what the mind does, after all—and gently turn my attention back to my mantra. This back-and-forth between thinking and focusing isn't failure. Corralling my wayward mind is part of the practice, and it's beneficial for intent for two reasons: it gives me the opportunity to observe my thoughts and gain insight into myself, and by noticing that I'm thinking and returning my attention to my mantra, I'm slowly but surely training my mind to settle down.

I sit for fifteen minutes, much of which I spend wrangling my wandering mind, which seems intent on zipping around like an amped-up toddler: *What should we have for dinner? Where is my pink sweater? I can't forget to call my mom!* Even so, when my iPhone gently chimes to let me know the time is up, I open my eyes feeling relaxed and calm. I take a deep breath and stretch, and then reach for my journal. While my mind is clear and present, I jot down some notes on my intents for the future:

> *July 24. I want to be present for my life—to wring as much joy out of it as I can and also face the sadness and setbacks with authenticity and grace. I want to be present for my*

daughters, Sumant, my parents, my friends, and for myself. My intents for the year:

Family. I want to connect with those who mean the most to me, to truly enjoy our time together and to feel grateful for what I have.

Balance. I want to figure out what it means for me and what it will take to find it.

Health. I want to commit to a regular fitness program, reduce sugar in my diet, and eat better overall—not only because I want to lose weight (although that would be a happy result) but also because I want to be healthy and treat my body with respect. I want to commit to physical activities that make me feel connected spiritually and full emotionally. I also want to pay attention to my sleep, because I know I'm a better person—I make better choices and I'm easier to get along with—when I'm well-rested.

Fun. I want to identify the activities that make me laugh and bring me joy, and bring them into my life on a regular basis.

Purpose. I want to reignite my passion for what I do every day, whether as a parent, a wife, or a businesswoman. I want to find the meaning in my everyday activities so I do them with a sense of respect and clarity—giving my all to bettering myself, my family, and the world I live in.

Intent. I want to feel energetic, creative, joyful, centered, and inspired, and to the best of my ability, bring more love into my life and the lives of those I touch.

Not a short list, but it is a doable one, I think. I feel so good—centered, calm, *whole*. And to think I've been stressing and spinning out for years when this healing practice of meditation has been just a few breaths away all along.

When I began meditating as a child, I was an outlier among my peers. My dad publicly advocated meditation, but his perspective on it was seen as out there on the fringe by the mainstream media. One particular memory of that time stands out. It was the early nineties, when I was in college, and I was at an airport waiting for a flight. As I browsed the magazine rack, I saw a comic image of my dad on the cover of a magazine. My father's head was overly large, and he was sitting in the lotus position, meditating (maybe even levitating) with eight arms in contorted positions around him. He was holding snake oil in one hand, incense in another. The message was clear: meditation is loony.

Despite all that, the practice was an incredible gift that I cherished. I knew from experience that it healed, that it made me feel more secure, more centered and happier. When I was a teenager, it was a tool that helped me know who I was in the precarious world of adolescents. Sitting in stillness helped me feel connected to something bigger than my own daily drama, and it gradually instilled in me a quiet confidence in my own voice and perspective.

In the last ten years, meditation has become trendy in the United States, a transformation that never fails to make me smile. While many people are "discovering" meditation today, the practice has extraordinarily deep historical and spiritual roots. Some historians speculate that early humans meditated by staring into the flames of their life-giving fires, and the practice, which was popularized by the Buddha in 500 BC, is mentioned in Indian scriptures from five thousand years ago. You don't need to be spiritual to meditate, but for those of us who believe in something greater than ourselves, the practice can serve as a way of connecting to the divine, whether for you that's called God or consciousness or the universe. When I meditate, I feel part of that larger *something* that connects us and makes us one with all living beings.

The benefits I've experienced with meditation—greater clarity and focus, reduced stress, enhanced insights into myself—have been fully validated by science in the past couple of decades. Research has shown that these aren't blessings bestowed upon a lucky few. They're available to anyone who takes the time to commit to the practice, and the more you meditate, the greater the benefit.

Research on meditation began in earnest in the early nineties, when the Dalai Lama invited Richard Davidson, a neuroscientist at the University of Wisconsin, to go to Dharamsala, India, and interview monks who had been meditating for years; since then, Davidson and his colleagues have studied dozens of Buddhists, including everyone from novices to those who've been practicing regularly. The findings from this unusual body of research suggest that meditating can actually alter the structure and function of the brain—the more you do it, the more the brain changes. Using functional magnetic resonance imaging, fMRI, the researchers found that experienced meditators have stronger activation of brain areas related to attention than novice meditators. Simply put, they can focus more easily and cut through the distractions and chaos of everyday life. When it comes to incubating intents, which requires focused attention, no skill is more essential. Conversely, those who've been practicing the longest (an average of forty-four thousand hours) actually have *less* activation in those brain regions, indicating that their ability to sustain attention requires less cognitive exertion. One explanation is that their hours of practice have given them the ability to focus their minds with little effort—it has become second nature.

As I read about these studies, it occurs to me that I've been living in the present, but I haven't been *awake* in the present. My mind is always elsewhere—rehashing things that happened the day before or worrying about things that might (and might not) happen in the future. The result: I misplace my keys, my wallet, my phone. I tell friends the same story twice, and often forget to tell Sumant about a school event he needs to attend—then I get annoyed with him for not showing up. Perhaps one reason I feel my life lacks meaning and purpose is because my mind lacks focus. I'm so busy that I no longer take the time to think about what I want—to incubate my desires, to live daily in the way that I know gives me peace and happiness. Could becoming more attentive to the present help me find things to savor in my everyday experience—things I've been missing because I've been moving too fast?

I'm also moodier these days, and the meditation research provides hope on that front as well. Preliminary evidence suggests that longtime practitioners may be less emotionally reactive than the rest of us. In response to emotional sounds (a baby cooing, a woman screaming) they show less activation than novices do in the amygdala, the part of the brain that fires up when you're afraid or worried. In other words, meditation can help you gain control of your reactions and emotions. That makes sense. Meditation and other contemplative practices are powerful stress relievers, calming the nervous system and reducing levels of the stress hormone cortisol. When you're less stressed you're less reactive. Instead of spinning around like a whirling dervish—my typical MO—you're more thoughtful and better equipped to make reasonable choices. Sign me up.

> I'm so busy that I no longer take the time to think about what I want—to incubate my desires, to live daily in the way that I know gives me peace and happiness.

Dr. Dan Siegel, a clinical professor of psychiatry at UCLA, helps me dig deeper into the value of incubation during a conversation in his office, which, it turns out, is not far from where I live in Santa Monica. I reached out to him after reading his fantastic book *Mindsight,* in which he describes "openness" as being receptive to whatever comes to our awareness, without clinging to preconceived ideas of how things should be. It struck me then as it does now that openness is a helpful mind-set for incubating intents. And Siegel himself is nothing if not open. He welcomes me warmly and seems eager to hear about my book and to talk about intention. I realize that greeting people with such openness is a way of establishing a personal connection within moments—and it requires the presence of mind I'm hoping to develop through meditation.

Openness is important for incubation, too, because unless you're open and receptive, you'll miss important insights and connections between various aspects of your life that might provide clues to new sources of meaning and purpose. I realize I can be open only when I come from a quiet place, when I let go of the constant chatter, when I quit analyzing every comment and situation.

Dr. Siegel tells me that openness enables us to see things clearly. "We let go of expectations and receive things as they are, rather than trying to make them how we want them to be. It gives us the power to recognize restrictive judgments and release our minds from their grip." This comment strikes a chord. I know my mind is filled with restrictive judgments, and I'm hoping that the awareness I'm working on now will help me notice and decipher them.

"Self-knowing awareness not only helps you understand your own life and your purpose but also helps you relate more compassionately with others. When you're awake in your mind you can be a better friend, a better spouse, and a better parent," he says. "Parenting is really about creating intention and being fully present in the moment with kindness and compassion."

I tell Dr. Siegel about my book and explain that I'm working on incubating intents. "Incubating is like my idea of response flexibility, which really means pause before you act and consider your options. Incubating is response flexibility writ large—it's pausing to figure out your life course," he says. "It's the first step in acknowledging that you're here for a reason and trying to figure out and honor what that reason is."

> "Self-knowing awareness not only helps you understand your own life and your purpose but also helps you relate more compassionately with others. When you're awake in your mind you can be a better friend, a better spouse, and a better parent."

By the time I hug Dr. Siegel good-bye, my heart is full of gratitude and my mind is spinning with weighty thoughts. What is the reason I'm here? How can I honor that reason?

It's a question we all should ponder. Why are you here? What purpose can we serve? What greater good can we do? How can we give our best to the world and leave it a little better than we found it?

I'm trying to meditate one day but urgent thoughts keep intruding. *Don't forget to take cupcakes to school! I have to prepare for my presentation for the wellness conference! Is that lunch with the other moms tomorrow or next week?* My to-do list is stampeding through my mind, trampling any chance of tranquillity. But I know from experience that the onslaught of thoughts is not a bad thing—the fact that my mind is racing actually reassures me that sitting for these ten minutes is exactly what I need to be doing.

I open my eyes and allow myself to think just about my list. Within minutes, my heart is pounding and I can practically feel the stress hormone cortisol shooting through my veins. What's making me stressed? I feel overwhelmed, yes, but there's more: I feel . . . guilty. Guilty that I'm taking on too much, guilty that I'm not doing anything well, guilty that I'm giving short shrift to my kids, Sumant, my job. *And what about you, Mallika?* a quiet voice asks. *How are you shortchanging yourself?*

I think about what Dr. Siegel said about restrictive judgments. As restrictive judgments go, guilt is near the top for many moms. I've been reading Sheryl Sandberg's book *Lean In,* and I recall something she says on the topic: "Guilt management can be just as important as time management for mothers." Guilt management? What a concept! I grab the book from my bedside table and reread the chapter on having it all. Toward the end, she says, "Instead of perfection we should aim for sustainable and fulfilling. The right question is not, 'Can I do it all?' but 'Can I do what's most important for me and my family?'"

As I read those words, it occurs to me that instead of feeling anxious about the activities on my schedule, I could just say no. One word, two letters, enormous power. Being overscheduled and stressed isn't helping me incubate my intents—not just because I don't have enough time to devote to it but also because I don't have enough energy. I feel too depleted to do the deep work I want to do to proceed with this project. Yet I realize now that I don't have to volunteer for everything at school. I can be more particular about which speaking engagements I accept. I can tell my friends every once in a while that I can't participate in mom lunches. The thought is both liberating and scary all at once. I believe in the power of yes—in embracing opportunities that come along. But perhaps I need to bring more mindfulness to my yeses and deploy no more often.

It's a challenge every woman I know should consider. With more downtime, we all can become more mindful and incubate more effectively. And doing so can help us recognize the moments when we need to say no—for ourselves, for our families, for our sanity—and embrace the occasions when we want to say *Yes!*

As the days go by, I try to be choosier about the activities I volunteer for and the invitations I accept, and already I can see that it has opened up time. The sky hasn't fallen and no one is accusing me of being a terrible mom. At least not yet. As my stress eases ever so slightly, I start to incubate ideas for the activities I want to embrace. What will bring me relaxation, fulfillment, joy? To what and whom should I say yes?

I make a list of things that sound appealing: A walk with a friend on the beach. Breakfast with Sumant before our busy day begins. Sad as it sounds, it's not easy to come up with ideas for things I'd enjoy doing.

For inspiration, I look around at my friends to see what the happiest among them like to do, and one activity stands out: yoga. They all love it, and it's often topic number one after we drop off our kids at their school. They talk about what classes they're taking, what teachers they like, what times they go. The conversation never fails to make me uncomfortable, as I have a difficult relationship with yoga. That is a nice way of saying I suck at it.

I don't mind being a novice in some activities, but yoga is a different story. Because of my father, everyone expects me to be a limber yogi. The truth is, I can't even do a decent downward-facing-dog position. When one of my dearest friends, Cara, suggests we get a group of women together to do a class a couple of times a week, I actually roll my eyes.

"What, are you not into yoga?" she asks, sounding shocked.

My ambivalence toward the practice has been my hidden shame; until this moment, not even my good friends knew about it.

"Not particularly," I say, adding guiltily, "though, I probably should be."

"Well, I'd love it if you'd join us," says Cara, adding, "It doesn't matter what level you are. It'll be super casual. And yoga isn't about being good or bad. It's about finding your limits and tuning in to yourself. It's like meditation for the body."

"I'll think about it," I promise her. And I do. Later that day after my meditation, my mind calm and clear, I make a pro and con list.

The cons: I'm not good at it, and that makes me
uncomfortable and embarrassed.

The pros: Yoga fulfills several of my intents. It's a
healthy physical activity that will help me feel
more energetic and, I hope, less stressed. And
doing it with Cara and other moms could be fun
and would give me a nice way to connect and
share a meaningful experience with friends.

Am I willing to let go of my ego so I can experience
something that's healthy and could bring me greater joy?
Several months ago, the answer might have been different.
But now that I'm committed to examining my choices and
enriching my life, I see there's only one answer: yes.

The next day when I see Cara I say, "Count me in for
the class."

"Yay!" she says, giving me a hug. "You won't regret it."

I've started meditating in the early afternoon, before I pick
up the girls from school. It's a time when I'm typically winding up work and puttering around aimlessly. Slipping meditation into that time slot is a nice way to mark the end of
my official workday and the beginning of my mom duties.
Also, doing it at the same time every day makes it easier to
squeeze in; it's gradually becoming an automatic part of my
life, like brushing my teeth or washing my face.

But the process of meditating remains difficult, not like

what I'd experienced in the past during my practice. Perhaps life is more complicated now that I have more responsibilities? There are times when my mind is so churned up that access to any sort of tranquillity feels nearly impossible, and dishearteningly few sessions yield aha moments. I remind myself over and over again that it's OK to have these thoughts, and that meditative sitting is worth it no matter what. Focusing the mind, letting go of my thoughts—these are good and valuable things in and of themselves. Besides, it's called "practice" for a reason. There is no end point at which you've become as good as you can get or achieved everything you possibly can—even for Buddhist monks who've been doing it for years.

Buddhists call the novice meditator's inability to focus "monkey mind" because our thoughts jump around like an amped-up chimp. Jack Kornfield, an author and Buddhist teacher, uses a dog analogy. Meditation, he says, is like training a puppy.

"You put the puppy down and say, 'Stay.' Does the puppy listen? It gets up and it runs away. You sit the puppy back down again. 'Stay.' And the puppy runs away over and over again. Sometimes the puppy jumps up, runs over, and pees in the corner or makes some other mess." He says our minds are the same as we learn to meditate—and I can relate as I relearn it. My mind jumps around and chases its tail; if it could, I'm certain it would get up and pee in the corner.

The lesson, he says, is that in training the mind, just as

in training a puppy, you have to start over and over again, which requires compassion. I'm good at showing compassion to my kids, Sumant, even to all my friends and family. But compassion for myself? Not so much. So I add that to the list of my challenges as I move forward. If I miss a day of meditation or have a so-so session, I need to remind myself it is no big deal. Incubation takes time and patience. There's always tomorrow.

Yoga class with Cara brought me the biggest surprise: enjoyment. By the second class, I didn't care that I wasn't as limber as the rest of the women, nor did anyone else. They were all focused on their own challenges. With my ego out of the way, I was able to engage on a whole new level, bringing my awareness and attention to my body and mind as I moved through the postures. I realized then that the physical aspect of yoga was a needed ingredient for my own incubation practice. Focusing on my breath, releasing tension in my neck, stretching, being still in a pose. The physical benefits of yoga brought awareness and expansiveness into my life in a way that meditation brought stillness and silence. It gave me a new way of being in the present moment, of setting a physical intent and being patient as I eased into a pose. I realized that sometimes a small adjustment made the posture easier, and in so doing I saw new ways of achieving the same goal in meditation. But yoga, too, requires patience. I didn't perfect my downward-facing dog immediately, but it did start to feel more comfortable as I adjusted to what felt best for me. And like meditation, yoga began yielding insights almost immediately.

One day, perhaps a month into our weekly classes, while standing in the tree pose, I realized I was less wobbly than usual. More rooted. And it occurred to me that finding balance in my physical being is an apt metaphor, maybe even practice for, finding balance in the rest of my life—between the yeses and the nos, between guilt and gratification, between doing for others and doing for myself. Balance is always, by definition, a dicey prospect—difficult to maintain, easy to lose. Until now, I've been feeling guilty (there it is again) about the fact that my life feels out of whack. As if I should always be perfectly poised and centered. But that day in yoga I realized we all go through phases of feeling adrift, shaky, and unsure of ourselves—and that's not necessarily a bad thing. Change doesn't happen when we feel confident, strong, and rooted. The blessing of uncertainty is that it gives us the nudge we need to dig deep—to incubate and reflect on what we want—and to find the courage to carve out a different path.

INTENTIONAL LIVING:
REFLECTIONS AND PRACTICES

Incubation is about tapping into silence and stillness, about settling the constant chatter in our minds to feel connected to the deeper spirit that lies within all of us. Incubation also fosters creativity as we break out of our normal patterns of doing things and glimpse new possibilities.

1. Go for a weekly hike or walk in nature. Don't listen to music or any other audio recording. Instead, savor the sounds of nature.

2. Set aside a minimum of fifteen minutes for agenda-free time today. Choose to listen to a few of your favorite songs, play the piano, dance … whatever brings you joy.

3. If you have never practiced yoga, sign up for a yoga class and try it. If you are an avid yoga practitioner, try your next class without music or any other stimulation. Or try another form one day. Truly pay attention to your breath and the openness that yoga brings to your mind and body.

4. If yoga is not for you, find another activity that incorporates movement and mindfulness—Tai Chi, Qigong, or even a dance class. Pay attention to how your mind reacts to the movement of your body.

INTENT PRACTICE: MEDITATION

The approach to basic meditation is simple.

- Set an alarm clock for five minutes. Choose a gentle sound, such as softly rung bells or sounds of nature—birds chirping or the like.
- I recommend twenty minutes, twice a day, as an ideal time to meditate—once in the morning and once in the late afternoon. But, if this is your first time or if you've not practiced in a while, try just five minutes, once a day. You can add an additional five minutes each week as you become more familiar with the practice of sitting. And if you can't do it each day, no guilt piling on is allowed!
- If you want, you can create a meditation space. Altars or candles, while not necessary, can be helpful in setting the stage and creating the mind-set and mood for change. Choose photos, statues, crystals, or items from nature—a leaf, a flower, a beautiful stone or shell—that symbolize change. Arrange them in a way that's pleasing or meaningful to you.
- Choose a sitting posture that's comfortable—in a chair or on the floor on a meditation pillow.

You want to be relaxed but alert, so lying down isn't a good idea. Sit up straight, with your spine erect, but allow your body to feel at ease, like a silk jacket draped over a hanger. Take a few deep breaths, make any minor adjustments to your posture you need in order to feel comfortable, then close your eyes and allow your breath to settle into its natural rhythm.

- Rest your attention on the breath as it enters and leaves your body.
- When your mind wanders, simply notice what has happened and gently return your attention to your breathing.
- Here is a very simple meditation that uses "I am" to help keep your mind from wandering too much.
  - Close your eyes.
  - Take a few deep breaths to connect with your body and settle into your surroundings.
  - As you breathe in, mentally say *"I."*
  - Pause.
  - As you breathe out, mentally say *"am."*
  - Continue this process.
  - *I*

    am.

    I

    am.

- After a few minutes, stop repeating this phrasing.
- Take a few deep breaths again, and pause to feel whatever sensations you are experiencing in your body.
- When you are ready, open your eyes.
- Keep a journal at hand to write down any thoughts, insights, or observations you take away from the experience.

THREE

NOTICE

While chatting on the phone with my friend Romi one day I confess my concerns about my weight, my poor eating habits, my overreliance on caffeine and sugar, and my lack of exercise.

"I get it," she says. "I'm feeling the same."

In fact, she says, she is about to book a week-long retreat at a challenging fitness and wellness resort in Malibu.

"Maybe you should join me," she suggests.

My knee-jerk response is no. Not just no. *Hell, no.*

I'm not a fitness-resort kind of person. I'm not a course type of person. I've never even attended a full seminar of my dad's at the Chopra Center. But I bite my tongue and instead say, "I'll definitely consider it."

My return to meditation has helped me improve my ability to be more considered in my responses, and to notice my reactions to my environment and circumstances. Notice is an important part of living with intent—to notice internally what is happening in your body, with your emotions, and in your reactions to situations. But a key piece of noticing is also paying attention to external opportunities and coincidences—and once I've had some time to reflect, I see that Romi's offer is a prime opportunity to gain greater understanding of my health issues.

I click on the resort's website. It's expensive and extravagant, as I had feared—not the kind of thing I ordinarily go in for. But its immersive week-long program would give me lots of what I need: an opportunity to learn about healthy eating, get clarity on some of my habits, and jump-start my exercise routine.

I text Romi: LET'S DO IT.

That's how I find myself one gorgeous fall day puffing up a steep, narrow trail in the mountains of Malibu, sweating madly and wondering what I've gotten myself into. It's day one of our retreat, and I'm already having second thoughts.

"You OK?" Romi asks as she slows down for me to catch up. Despite the fact that she's eight years older than I am, she's in far better shape.

I nod—though I'm far from certain I'll survive the week's challenges. In preparation, I've tapered off from the usual caffeine—five cups of tea plus two double macchiatos with sugar every day—to a single, virtuous cup of tea, a huge accomplishment for me. In doing this, I notice I feel better; it sounds counterintuitive, but without so much caffeine I'm actually *less* tired, *more* focused. I've also been staying away from sugar, except for a splurge on a cupcake yesterday— one last desperate fling before going cold turkey. Fitness- wise I've done little to prepare, and that makes me nervous. What if I can't handle the exercise?

I'm not sure how I'll fare emotionally either. I've never spent this long away from my husband and kids, and it scares me. I'm concerned I'll miss them terribly. What if something happens while I'm gone? What if someone gets sick or needs me?

You're not on the moon, I remind myself as I force my weary legs up the trail.

By 7:45 that first night, we're all dead tired. "That was the longest day of my life," moans one of my fellow campers as we head to bed. Of the seventeen participants, sixteen are women, most of them in their forties or early fifties. Though most are fitter than I am, what I noticed today is that I'm not alone in this struggle. *All* the women have some dissat- isfaction with their daily lifestyle choices and want to make healthy changes, and all are walloped by day's end. In our defense, we've done more in thirteen hours than most of us do in a month: from an early-morning stretch class that included planks and downward-facing dogs, to two hikes and a full slate of afternoon classes (core strength, TRX [Total Body Resistance Exercise], abs, and yoga). No wonder we're tired.

Despite my fatigue, I feel happy about what I accomplished—an emotion that fades slightly as soon as I call home. Tara answers, and within minutes of hearing my voice, her mood goes from quiet to weepy to full-on sobbing. She's going through a hard time—a confluence of hormones and emotional sensitivity that leaves her feeling raw and wounded much of the time. Maybe she needs me at home. I feel my resolve to stay at the resort draining away like water from a bathtub.

I breathe deeply as we talk and fight the urge to say, "I'll be right there!" Then, just as we are about to hang up, I mention that I ate granola with almond milk for breakfast—and she bursts into hysterical laughter.

"No way! *You* ate that? I can't believe it!"

And just like that, she's her usual, happy self. Some of her emotional drama, I suddenly realize, is for my benefit. She hates when I'm away, even for a quick overnight, and knows exactly how to make me feel guilty about it. It's a good lesson. I don't always need to take her adolescent drama so seriously. And it's a good reminder of the reason I'm there. If the idea of my eating a healthy meal is completely outlandish to my daughter, what does that say about my usual diet and the food messages I'm sending to my kids?

The week flies by in a flurry of fitness classes, nutrition

education, massages, and vegetarian meals—food that I actually grow to enjoy, to Tara's and Leela's continued confusion and delight. By the last day, I feel fitter, stronger, slimmer, and better prepared to make healthy choices for me and my family. I've lost seven pounds and several inches. I haven't had any sugar and completely weaned myself from caffeine for seven days and notice the benefits; my mind is clearer and I have far more energy. Despite my worries on day one, I not only survived this retreat—I feel great.

On the last day, we write letters to ourselves, and the staff promises to mail them to us in six months. As I seal my envelope, I say a little prayer to the universe: *When I receive this letter, may I be closer to living my intents.*

Our final hike is a six-mile trek to the highest peak in the Santa Monica Mountains. I'm still at the back of the pack, and I feel a twinge of disappointment. A part of me had hoped I'd be able to keep up with the faster group. But instead of feeling defeated, I let go of my inner competitiveness and simply enjoy the moment. The warm air, the beautiful blue sky, the jagged rocks, the newfound strength in my legs and lungs are worth relishing.

As I approach the hike's highlight, a massive Buddha-shaped boulder known as Balance Rock, I slow and then stop. Poised precariously on a steep point, it looks dangerously unstable from every angle, as if its weight weren't evenly distributed and it could topple over with the next strong gust. Yet somehow it has found the sweet spot—the place where it can hold steady, through wind and rain, in spite of its risky foundation.

Honestly, there couldn't be a more perfect metaphor for what I'm trying to achieve during my life at the moment: elusive, improbable balance. And here is a graphic illustration of how it looks—implausible yet solid—wrought from the simple grandeur of Mother Nature herself.

Thank you, universe, I think with a chuckle, as I continue on my way.

Later, after I've finished the hike, I learn that the fast hikers were moving so quickly they missed the rock altogether. The journey really *is* the destination—if we slow down enough to pay attention. When we slow down to notice, the universe gives us the signs we need. I feel certain that Balance Rock was put in my path for a reason—a sign that I'm heading in the right direction, the one that will eventually lead me to a fuller, richer life.

> When we slow down to notice, the universe gives us the signs we need.

The first night I'm at home, I drift off into a restless half sleep, and from among the random thoughts running through my mind, one jumps out. It's about our internal dialogues, and how noticing what we're thinking can help us shape our moods, our behavior, our interactions, and our lives. As kids, Gotham and I were instructed by our dad to notice our thoughts as well as to pay attention to how the words we utter affect us and those around us.

A dim lightbulb flickers on for me as I remember this. I've always known that self-awareness was critical for setting and fulfilling intents, which is why I consider noticing the second crucial step in the intent process.

In my semiconscious state, I tune in to my drifting thoughts. *I feel bloated. Maybe it's all the fiber I ate on the retreat. How did my friend land that great new job? Why her? What if I can't write my book? What if it sucks and people hate it? I really don't like the project we are consulting for from Intent right now. It doesn't dovetail at all with what I wanted to do with this company. Am I not in charge? Why do I feel as if I'm not in control of my own destiny?*

Whoa! Where'd the magic and calm of my retreat go? Is this really what's going on just below the surface of my consciousness all the time? It's as if someone has pulled back the curtain and given me a view of the cobwebby recesses of my psyche—and I don't like what I see. I'm slightly appalled by the darkness of my internal landscape, and I'm struck by the desire to close the curtain and forget I ever glimpsed what lay behind it. But denial isn't on the list of things I've signed up to do this year. I realize that the retreat, while a lovely and helpful escape, wasn't part of the real world. What I need to do now is find my own retreat—the version that works for me—in my life at home. We all need to make moments for reflection, and create sacred spaces for aware-ness, to reconnect, to reenergize, and to recommit.

I don't want to escape my life; I want to enhance it. Noticing my thoughts—and how they affect everything about my day-to-day existence—is as good a place as any to start. I get out of bed and take my journal from a handbag, jotting down these words: *I'll continue to pay attention to my thoughts and notice how often they're negative.*

Then I grab Tolle's book *A New Earth* from my bedside table. In search of wisdom, I flip the pages and happen upon a subhead called "The Background Unhappiness":

> *Apart from the obvious ones such as anger, hatred and so on, there are other more subtle forms of negativity that are so common they are usually not recognized as such, for exam-ple, impatience, irritation, nervousness, and being "fed up." They constitute the background unhappiness that is many people's predominant inner state. You need to be extremely alert and absolutely present to be able to detect them. When-ever you do, it is a moment of awakening.*

In the days after the retreat, I keep a mental tally of my self-talk, both during my meditation sessions and in my daily life—and I observe a number of things. For one, my conversations are littered with freighted language: *tired, too much to do, overwhelmed, rushing, busy, stressed, exhausted*. I hear myself lamenting that I don't have time to exercise, plan for dinner, pay the bills, or go grocery shopping; yet I somehow manage to find an hour or two to play silly video strategy games or read about a celebrity's latest antics on the Internet. I'm perpetually complaining about how busy I am, but at day's end I often look back and have no idea where the time went. My life is full of action and the veneer of having too much to do, yet I am rarely fulfilled. And I grouse and whine. I have become the Queen Complainer, the Empress Excuse-Maker. *Yuck.*

It's an uncomfortable realization but an important one that I must sit with more. A key piece of mindfulness is being a *nonjudgmental* observer—to notice without making judgments. I need to be able to recognize the thoughts that aren't so attractive if I want to minimize them and imbue my day with positive thoughts instead. As I make it a practice to notice my own thoughts, I realize I'm fairly patient with other people's failings, but it's far harder to accept my own. In fact, as I pay more attention to my thoughts, I notice that my impulse to self-chastise is almost reflexive. Even in the moment when I catch my mind veering in a negative direction, I start critiquing myself for being negative. I set the intent to notice the thoughts and let them go, releasing them, rather than holding on to them or analyzing them.

As the days go by I try to observe my internal experience

without denouncing it—and when I do become self-critical, I think, *Oh, that's interesting; now I'm judging*. Naming the behavior actually minimizes its emotional bite. And according to Dr. Siegel, there's a biological explanation for how that works. Research by his colleagues at UCLA shows that when you name an emotion or experience, it calms down the neural firing in the emotion-processing part of the brain known as the limbic system, the same site that revs up the fight-or-flight mechanism when we perceive a threat. It's happened to me many times before, particularly in the work environment when I am afraid of disappointing a client or investor. I create scenarios in my head about the complaints or anger, my blood pressure rises, my heart pounds. And yet nothing has even happened yet. I notice the symptoms and name my fear—I'm afraid of disappointing my client—and can breathe again before taking action.

When it comes to negative emotions, Siegel says, "You need to name it to tame it." I love that. As I practice the naming/taming technique, I notice that it has another benefit: it gives me some distance from my thoughts and helps me recognize that my mental chatter, even the ugly stuff, isn't an indictment of me as a person. It comes from my mind, but it doesn't define who I am.

> What do you notice when you sit back and listen to the voices in your head?

That's true for all of us. And it's time to let go of the judgment and shame our negative thoughts create. What do you notice when you sit back and listen to the voices in your head? Are you ready to accept them, let go of judgment, and then truly release them? Try it—one complaint or one self-criticism at a time.

As I continue to meditate and name/tame, I gradually get better at witnessing my mind in action. So I take another step and try to observe myself and the whole of my life, not just its internal landscape—and really *see* it, warts and all. The first thing I notice isn't surprising: I'm tired. Even if I sleep a solid nine hours at night, I slog through my days as if I'm carrying a backpack filled with bricks.

Despite my visit to the spa, and all that hiking and healthy eating, I'm still overweight and out of shape—not terribly so, but I'm not living up to my intents in this realm. My weekly yoga class continues—and I love it—but one class a week is not enough to make a huge improvement in my health. When I walk up hills and climb stairs, I still get slightly breathless. And when I reach into my closet one morning, I realize I've been avoiding some of my favorite clothes because I know they'll be too tight.

Once I start noticing, I can't stop. One day while I'm sitting in a business meeting, I realize I've developed a habit of crossing my arms and legs, a posture that doesn't exactly communicate openness and warmth. I take a moment to tune in to my body. It feels as if I'm physically trying to hold in my nervous energy and stress—and maybe even block out other people's ideas and energy. "Tightly wound" is the phrase that comes to mind. I've never been an uptight person. But it appears my body is mirroring what's happening in my mind. I consciously uncross my limbs and let them hang loose, and that simple action makes me feel relaxed, friendly, and a little more receptive. It's as if the cells in my body were telling my brain, *OK, stand down; the threat has passed*. But what threat?

My connections with people I care about aren't faring much better. Although I love my yoga class with my women friends, I've become detached from other friends in troubling ways. I've lost touch with some of my closest friends and narrowed my conversations with my husband to (a) complaining about my life or (b) negotiating the logistics of the kids' schedules. When he suggests that the kids and I go to San Francisco for the weekend to join him at a conference, I beg off, using my endless to-do list as my excuse. I'm also irritated that he would ask and put pressure on me when he knows I just want to relax on the weekend. Then I have a terrible thought: I don't really have that much to do! It occurs to me that I'm trying to make him feel guilty. But for what? I have no idea. Maybe I'm resentful that he has more independence to spend his time as he pleases than I do. Maybe I feel bad about myself, so I want him to suffer too.

My days of noticing reveal more and more. I snap at my kids frequently, and I'm forever saying *Hurry up!* I get frustrated, especially at Leela, who has a particularly leisurely pace of eating, walking, and talking. But my impatience with her causes a pang of remorse every time I snap at her. One of the things I love most about her is her deliberate approach. It's admirable and sweet and uniquely *her*. I envy her ability to march to her own drummer.

Could it be that she frustrates me because I feel unable to march to mine?

Noticing my "background unhappiness," as Tolle calls it, is one thing. Seeing that it's affecting my most valued relationships is another. I need to find a way to turn myself around.

I'm scrolling through posts on Facebook when I notice a link to an article on gratitude. *That's interesting. Gratitude has been in the back of my mind for a bit.* As messages from the universe go, it's a quiet one. But I click on the link anyway because the topic speaks to me. The link opens a piece from the *New York Times* that mentions the work of psychologists Robert Emmons and Michael McCullough, who have conducted studies on thankfulness. Their seminal work shows that keeping a gratitude journal, in which you list five things every day for which you feel grateful, can make you happier and more optimistic. The people who participated in the study also said they had fewer physical problems and exercised more. I think about my cousin Kanika. Before they begin eating dinner each evening, Kanika; her husband, Sarat; and their two daughters, Aanya and Mira, say three things for which they're thankful. She swears it makes everyone more polite, more open, more connected.

Intrigued, I go on Amazon and order Emmons's book *Thanks!* He says that in the short term, on a day-to-day basis, feeling grateful can enhance feelings of love, forgiveness, joy, and enthusiasm. If you make gratitude a habit, and it becomes a part of your default mind-set, you can experience all those life-enhancing emotions as well as protect yourself from some of the more noxious stuff, such as envy, resentment, greed, and bitterness. A sample from *Thanks!*:

> *Gratitude, we have found, maximizes the enjoyment of the good—our enjoyment of others, of God, or our lives. . . . Gratitude elevates, it energizes, it inspires, it transforms. People are moved, opened, and humbled through experiences and expressions of gratitude. Gratitude provides life with meaning by encapsulating life as a gift.*

How often do I think of my current life as a gift? I've always valued gratitude, and I try to express my appreciation to my colleagues at work. But I'm not as diligent about it with my husband and kids, nor am I particularly good at regularly counting my blessings—which seems crazy because I have so, so much to be grateful for in my life. Reading Emmons's work makes me realize that gratefulness isn't just a worthy practice; it's also powerful *medicine*—possibly even an antidote to my toxic mind-set.

There is a clear line connecting how our thoughts affect our emotions, our emotions affect our choices, and our choices shape our experiences. And we have the power to shift the whole paradigm—and, according to Siegel's work, possibly even change our brains.

Every time we have a thought, he says, certain neurons in our brains fire. If I have the same negative thoughts over and over, I strengthen the links between those specific neural pathways. Doing this makes it easier and easier for my brain to return to that well-worn path. But if I shift my thoughts toward gratitude—or hope or happiness or love—I can actually strengthen the circuitry of well-being. In other words, by consciously choosing to focus on the emotions that dovetail with my intents, I can physically alter the structure of my brain so it's more in line with who I want to be—happier, more thoughtful, calmer, and more compassionate.

As part of my noticing project, I decide to try it. I start jotting down a list of things I'm thankful for—and every day the list grows, . . . and grows, and grows! My wonderful daughters. Loving, involved parents. A supportive husband. Interesting, inspiring friends. Financial security. A top-notch education. Fairly robust physical health. My kids' teachers. Our goofy dog, Yoda. And those are the biggies. Before long I start noticing smaller things too: The gorgeous weather in Southern California. The lovely produce at the farmers' market. The brilliant purple trees in our neighborhood. The businessman who took the time to hold the door for me. The slant of the afternoon sun through our kitchen window. All of these I jot down, and as I write the words, I take a few minutes to let the feeling of gratitude sink into my mind and heart. I really feel it. I marinate in it.

And in those moments, the sticky windows of my mind are thrown open and the sunlight pours in.

Being more grateful reminds me of a lesson my father taught Gotham and me when we were young. When we complained about homework or chores, he liked to remind us that our thoughts shape our reality.

"If you pay attention, you'll notice it in your own life. If you think studying is boring, it will be boring. If you think it's fun, it will be fun. Your choice," he'd tell us.

When we were being particularly annoying and bickering nonstop, he'd set a rule: no criticizing, condemning, or complaining. "Notice how that makes you feel," he'd suggest.

Competitive kids that we were, Gotham and I made a game of it, seeing if we could force the other person to complain first. One of my brother's favorite tricks was to barge into my room without knocking, hoping I would complain to my mom about what a painful pest he was. I couldn't, of course, because I'd lose the game. (As a parent, I now see the stealthy brilliance in my father's strategy. Here was a chance to teach us a valuable, mood-altering life skill, and at the same time curtail sibling squabbling. Genius!)

And it worked—not only to help us get along but also to transform our moods. On the days when Gotham and I were challenging ourselves not to complain, we had more fun together. We ended up laughing about silly things, being kinder to each other, seeing our problems from a more positive perspective.

Somewhere between adolescence and adulthood, I lost that early lesson. Maybe some innate pessimism kicked in, or I'd learned over the years that it's easier to complain than to look on the bright side. In any case, now I vow to reclaim it. So I start playing my own private version of the No Complaining game. When I'm stuck in a long, slow checkout line at the grocery store and feel myself becoming irritated with the woman in front of me who is chatting with the checker and digging through her purse for her checkbook, I notice it, then think, *What can I be grateful for in this moment?* A quick glance in my cart is enough to give me an answer. What I see is abundance—beautiful pears, strawberries, and apples; delicious goat cheese; my favorite kale for salad. When I look back at the woman, I notice she's elderly—older than I had thought. In my irritation I hadn't really seen her. Now I see that her hands are shaky as she scribbles her check, her gait a little unsteady as she toddles off. Suddenly I feel tender toward her—and happy that she can still get to the grocery store and be self-sufficient. It's not easy getting old in our go-go-go culture. I smile at the checker, who was tolerant and kind with the woman. "Thank you for being so patient," I say. And she lights up. "I love talking to people," she says. "It's the best part of my job. Otherwise, I'm just mindlessly going through the motions. Connecting with people is what it's all about."

Another day I'm running late for a meeting and instantly start beating myself up. *Why are you so stupid? Why didn't you just leave the house a little earlier? Why didn't you take a better route?* Then I notice my thoughts. *Uh-oh,* I think. *There I go, criticizing myself again.* Instead of berating myself, I think through the situation and tell myself it's no big deal. What's ten minutes one way or the other? But when I arrive—late, as I'd expected—and look around the room at the faces of the people who are gathered, I realize why I was so stressed. I wasted their time. And that's disrespectful. For me, it's not so much about being punctual or tardy, but rather it's about being considerate of people I care about. I want to honor my commitments and my relationships. And like the checker at Whole Foods, those are things I value. So I offer a sincere apology without the buffer of some trumped-up excuse (a tactic I've resorted to in the past). The tension in the room lifts, everyone smiles, I feel good about owning my bad behavior—and relieved that I've been forgiven.

The incident reminds me of something I read about gratitude and social interactions in Emmons's book, so when I return home I flip through it and find this: "*Naikan* is a practice of self-reflection that can help us 'see the reciprocal quality of relationships.'" Emmons quotes Gregg Krech, who wrote *Naikan: Gratitude, Grace, and the Japanese Art of Self-Reflection*: "If we are not willing to see and accept those events in which we have been the source of others' suffering, then we cannot truly know ourselves or the grace by which we live."

I'm stopped by the phrase *the grace by which we live*. I think about where the grace in my life comes from—the true blessings—and notice that it's mostly from other people, the friends and family who give my life meaning, of course, and the many nameless people I interact with during the day: the guy who lifted my carry-on bag into the overhead bin on the plane not long ago; the little boy who ran after me to return the car keys I'd unknowingly dropped while walking down the street. Even the drivers who give way so I can exit the freeway when I need to. To fulfill my intent to be there for friends and family, and the many strangers I come in contact with, I need to be grateful not only for the gifts they provide but also conscious about both the gifts I provide them and the ways in which I wound them, anger them, and disappointment them. It's a tall order. One I can't hope to perfectly fill. But the idea of seeing my interactions in the context of mutual support and gratitude strikes a chord deep within my soul.

We all have so many things to be grateful for—and they're often the last things we think about. I believe we should try to think about those things every day. What are you grateful for? What are the small things you take for granted that make your life special, more vibrant, and more magical—or just plain easier?

Whether because of my heightened awareness of the things and people I'm grateful for or my private moratorium on complaining, I'm feeling somewhat more sanguine after several weeks—less stressed, more centered, less negative, more hopeful. I'm one step closer to living with intent. I feel more sanguine than I have in a while when I fly to New York City to interview Caryl Stern, president and CEO of the United States Fund for UNICEF. I put Caryl on my list of interviewees after I heard her speak about her book, *I Believe in Zero*, in Los Angeles. In the book she shares stories of her travels and explains her dizzying goal: to reduce preventable childhood deaths from eighteen thousand a day to zero.

To me, Caryl's life is the definition of living with

intent—every day she is focused on helping children in need. What higher purpose can one have? When I asked during our interview, "What is the hardest part of your job?" I assumed she would say something about witnessing the ravages of poverty, war, and hunger on innocent children. After some thought, Caryl replied that it was leaving her kids, ages eleven and fourteen, when she had to travel for long periods of time. I realized that even those who seem to be working on a loftier plane are often dealing with the same personal issues as the rest of us. She may be saving the world, but she is a mom first.

I meet Caryl in her office in the UNICEF building near Wall Street. She's wearing a simple business suit, and her office is filled with books, photos, and neat stacks of paperwork. A suitcase sits by the side of her desk, evidence of her recent trip to Africa. I worry she'll be intimidating and remote, but she's so warm and welcoming we quickly fall into an easy conversation about how she came to be a leader in worldwide philanthropy.

When she was a senior in college, she tells me, she thought she was going to be a professional artist. "But I sensed that there was something else I was supposed to do with my life," she says. So she met with a career counselor who provided her with an exercise to help her gain some understanding of her innate strengths. As she tells me about it, I realize it's actually a powerful exercise in noticing.

"My counselor told me to buy a notebook and write

down everything I did for the next week. But my notes had to be detailed. I couldn't just say 'I ate dinner.' I had to include how I decided what I would eat. Did I decide, or did someone else? Did I shop . . . cook?"

By the time Stern met with her counselor again, the notebook was filled with information—and some insight into who she was. "Through that exercise, I learned that I was the organizer," Stern says. "If my friends and I went out on Friday night, it was because I called everyone and made it happen. I'd throw the dinner parties and head up the projects at school. The counselor said, 'This is the skill that comes to you naturally. This is what you're good at.' And I realized she was right. If you had told me my junior year of college that I'd be a CEO, I would have laughed in your face. But that exercise was a turning point in my evolution. It made me realize that I'd never thought about being a boss because I already was one. It was just what came naturally."

I explain to Stern that in India there's the concept of dharma—that we each have our own unique purpose. "I've struggled to find mine," I admit. "Do you believe you are living your true purpose?"

"Yes," she replies, "but it's not a simple one. I think I was born to try to make sense of the many losses in my family, many of whom died in the Holocaust. And the only way to make sense of it is to leave the world better than I found it. My relatives died and shouldn't have. I believe I'm here to try to make sure children don't die when we can prevent it from happening."

I notice how I'm feeling as I leave her office: calm, inspired, lighter. I love that she feels so connected to and guided by her family's history—or, as she put it, she's here to "sing her family's song." I've been noticing as the days have gone by that a big part of who I am and who I want to be is also shaped by my family history. I feel inspired by my parents and grandparents and motivated to live up to their examples. Every family has its own unique song. Notice what yours is, and sing it loudly and proudly.

> Every family has its own unique song. Notice what yours is, and sing it loudly and proudly.

While visiting my parents in La Jolla for the weekend, I have some rare quiet time with my father, and I decide to share some of what I'm going through. It's an unusual choice for me. While I often tap my father for writing and career advice, my mom is the one I confide in about my emotional struggles and vulnerability. It's always been that way. So when I start to open up to him about my challenges, I feel vaguely uncomfortable. The irony of the situation isn't lost on me. People around the world come to my father with their problems, but here I am feeling embarrassed about sharing my innermost thoughts with him—my own flesh and blood. Yet I sense that he can help, so I forge ahead.

I tell him I'm exhausted, that I don't feel good in my body, that I feel as if I have little control over the pace of my days, that I want to be of more service to others. He looks utterly bewildered and more than a little worried.

"I'm fine, Papa," I assure him. "It's just that something is missing. It's not about happiness or unhappiness. It's something more subtle."

I can practically see him shift from dad mode to Deepak mode. He brings up Daniel Siegel's work and shows me Siegel's Healthy Mind Platter for Optimal Brain Matter, created with David Rock, cofounder of the NeuroLeadership Institute.

As we talk about my well-being, we break it down into bite-size categories such as sleep, nutrition, exercise, relationships, work, intellectual stimulation, creativity and play, and spirituality. My dad encourages me to spend the next week noticing how I am doing in each category.

Thinking about Caryl Stern's exercise, I take time each day to notice how I am faring. I note how much I have slept each night, what I ate, how I used my downtime, how long I worked, whether I found time to meditate. In just a few days, I realize I'm thriving in exactly zero realms of my life. No wonder I feel so out of whack!

My first reaction: I feel bad about myself. But I notice

that self-defeating line of thinking and shift it before it goes too far. It's hard to do the things that are good for us, I remind myself. Whether it's eating kale chips instead of cookies, exercising religiously, practicing gratitude, or being mindful of our thoughts, we all struggle to keep ourselves on the right track. Noticing my thoughts will help me get there. But the goal isn't perfection. It's improvement. And as I think those comforting words I notice something wonderful: I feel hopeful.

INTENTIONAL LIVING:
REFLECTIONS AND PRACTICES

Noticing helps us tune in and get clarity on how we are feeling and reacting moment to moment—and why. It's a way of being mindful and present so we can see more clearly who we are and what we need in order to thrive. Also, noticing what is going on around us can give us inspiration and help us on our journey to achieving our intents.

1. Spend a day being mindful of your words—not complaining, criticizing another person or situation, or condemning another individual.
2. Keep a food journal to notice what you are eating every day. Make sure as well to include how much water or other liquids you drink.
3. Every night before going to sleep, write down or mentally review three things from the day for which you are grateful.

INTENT PRACTICE: YOUR
BALANCE WHEEL

- Sit in a warm, inviting place where you find inspiration and spend five to ten minutes meditating, then reflect on the Balance Wheel on page 84.
- Using the numbers 1 to 10, mark each section of the wheel:
  - 1–3: Suffering
  - 4–7: Struggling
  - 8–10: Thriving
- Don't think about it too much. Instead, let your intuition guide you and jot down your first response to each section.
- Which aspects of your life could use some attention? If you say "all," then join the crowd. As I said earlier, I wasn't thriving in any area when I began. So be kind to yourself and perhaps for now, just choose one.
- In a journal, begin to draft ideas about ways you could make small adjustments to your life—perhaps by setting a daily intent—to find greater balance. (We will expand more on Taking Action later in the book.)

MY BALANCE WHEEL

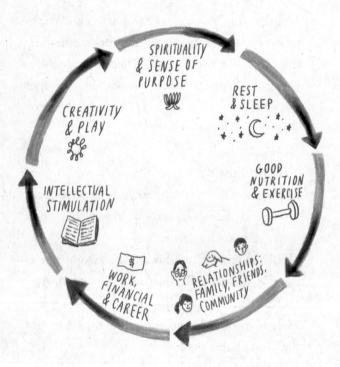

FOUR

TRUST

Amma, "the hugging saint," is in town, and my mother; sister-in-law, Candice; and I are invited to meet her. An Indian woman in her early sixties, Mata Amritanandamayi is a spiritual leader whose followers believe she is the embodiment of love and compassion. She spreads her love by traveling the world and embracing humanity—literally. Amma, which means "mother" in Hindi, has hugged more than thirty-four million people, many of whom say their time in her arms brings them wisdom, solace, and a feeling of connection to the divine. Some even say it changed their lives.

My friend Arielle Ford, for instance, met her soul mate within three weeks of asking Amma to send him to her. Another friend, a senior executive at Google, finds Amma's presence so healing he uses his vacation time to visit her no matter where she is in the world. Because I'm in the midst of a transformation and actively seeking direction, inspiration, and guidance, I'm eager to see what I might learn by paying a visit to this beloved guru. Maybe I, too, can learn to embrace life, and my purpose in it, more fully from Amma.

By the time we arrive at the hotel near Los Angeles International Airport where Amma and her entourage are set up, she's been hugging pilgrims for hours, and the lobby is still swarming with fans. The audience is varied: barefoot teens with long hair and tattoos, families with young children, suit-and-pumps–wearing professionals. All there for hugs from one woman. "If this many people need hugs so badly, maybe we should all just hug each other," I say to Candice, only half kidding.

Peeking into the conference room where Amma sits, I see what looks like more than a thousand people still waiting for their turn. Since the line to meet Amma is long, the VIP coordinator suggests we have dinner. "Given your 'Chopra' status, we'll try to get you in soon," he promises. His comment startles me, and gives me pause. On the one hand, I'm grateful. On the other, I'm put off. Status shouldn't matter in a place like this, should it?

The incident triggers memories of my youth, a large part of which I spent around Maharishi Mahesh Yogi, one of the first spiritual teachers to come to the West from India. He brought Transcendental Meditation to the United States, introducing it to thousands of people, including some, such

as the Beatles, who became high-profile advocates and followers.

After my father took up TM, Maharishi became his
teacher. I met him for the first time when I was thirteen, and
for the next decade he was a major influence in my life. My
brother, Gotham, and I sat for hours with him—sometimes
among crowds of thousands, other times with no one but
our parents. In the Indian tradition, gurus are teachers who
deserve the utmost respect, even more than your parents. As
a result, Maharishi held a place in our lives like no other.

When he spoke, I felt inspired, energized, motivated,
and at peace; and even though I was a shy child, I would run
to give him a rose when we said good-bye. He had a play-
ful spirit, and his delighted laugh upon receiving the token
always warmed my heart. His love and affection, along with
my parents', instilled in me a quiet confidence and taught
me to trust myself. A trust, it dawns on me, that I seem to
have lost over the years.

While I adored Maharishi, there was an aspect of his
entourage I didn't like—and I'm reminded of it as we're
waiting for Amma. His followers were constantly embroiled
in political maneuverings and power struggles; some visitors received preferential treatment while many did not. My
father was above all the machinations because he was close
with Maharishi, but I saw the artifice, drama, and postur-
ing nonetheless. What made me even more uncomfortable

was that some people in the movement elevated Gotham and me to a lofty status we in no way deserved. From their comments and deference, it was clear that they believed we were devout meditators and strict vegetarians—even that we were somehow enlightened. In reality, we were more interested in who shot J.R. on the TV show *Dallas* than in spiritual truths.

And, of course, I've seen people who have the same attitude toward my father. They flock to him as if he has the answers to all their problems. My dad is an amazing man with a brilliant mind, huge heart, and deep wisdom about spiritual issues, but he's just a human being. No matter how wise he is, he can't hold all the answers for someone else. No one can. The Buddhists say, "If you meet the Buddha on the road, kill him." Which simply means: be your own Buddha. Be who and what you are. Find your own truth. Don't look to others for answers. *Trust yourself.*

Recalling all this as I sit awaiting our time with Amma, I start to question why I've come. I long ago soured on the guru scene. But just as I'm getting cold feet, we're led to the conference room. Amma sits on a silk-draped chair in the middle of a stage. She wears a white *salwar kameez* (a traditional Indian outfit), the shawl covering her head. On her forehead is a large white-and-red *bindi*.

I watch Amma, fascinated. Her eyes shine with a brightness that reminds me of Maharishi, and when she's hugging someone, time stands still. I'm reminded of when my grandmother Maa hugged me when I was young. Maa's hugs were all encompassing. They were tight and certain and full of love. I close my eyes and recall the sensation of being in Maa's arms. And out of nowhere, I have the overwhelming urge to go home and hold Tara and Leela, to envelop them in an embrace that conveys endless love.

With that thought comes a tremendous sense of strength and peace. I don't want or need a guru. My uncertainty and my anchor, my questions and answers, my search and my truth all lie within my own soul. The same is true for every one of us. We may rely on others and turn to others for help, but ultimately our answers come from within.

As the Buddha is supposed to have said, *Be a lamp unto yourself. Look not for refuge in anyone but yourself.* No one else holds the secret to my happiness. What I need to do is trust my intuition and my ability to make choices that will make me happier, more balanced. What I need to do is trust myself.

"Do you want to get out of here?" I ask my mom and Candice. They nod, and we move toward the door. "I'll get you on the stage immediately," says our host, grabbing Candice and ushering her straight to Amma. Candice greets Amma warmly and tells her that everyone in our family sends love. Amma smiles, then envelops her in a long, deep embrace.

"It felt lovely and energizing," Candice reports afterward. When I get home, I hug Tara and Leela, rocking them in my arms. Lovely and energizing. I know just what she means. This love is deep and real and gives me a sense of peace. It's a feeling I trust without question.

The idea of trust surfaced again when I was writing down words that defined the intent process. Because intents are so deeply personal and unique—like an emotional fingerprint—they're impossible to fulfill without trusting your inner knowing, and trusting that the universe will guide the way.

> Because intents are so deeply personal and unique—like an emotional fingerprint—they're impossible to fulfill without trusting your inner knowing, and trusting that the universe will guide the way.

In order to discover and fulfill your intent, you need to trust not only your inner voice, or intuition, but also your body—and the universe. You need to allow yourself to be guided by intuition, by the quiet messages that come from inside—messages we often miss in the busyness of our everyday lives.

Sumant, an analytical left-brain thinker through and through, is skeptical when I talk about intuition. But even the great intellect Albert Einstein was a believer. "I believe in intuitions and inspirations . . . I sometimes *feel* that I am right, I do not *know* that I am," he said. Even the Bible refers to "the soft still voice within." That's the voice I'm trying to tune in to this year by meditating and noticing. That's the voice I know I can trust.

Does intuition really work? Surfing the Web one day, I type the phrase "science of intuition" into Google and get more than sixteen million hits. Wow. I guess I'm not the only one who's interested. I click through a few and find a fascinating study from the University of Iowa. Researchers there asked participants to play a card game, turning over one at a time from four different decks. By playing this "supposed" game of chance, they won money based on the number of high cards they drew. Although the participants didn't know it, the decks were stacked. Two of the four contained considerably more high-value cards. As the subjects played the game, a sensor measured the perspiration on their palms. And those sensors revealed something incredibly interesting. The players' palms started sweating after they'd drawn just ten cards. Even so, they didn't become consciously aware the decks were fixed till they'd turned over about fifty cards—and it took them another thirty flips to fully comprehend exactly how they were stacked. Their moist hands were warning them that something wasn't right long before they could perceive it consciously.

I've always thought of intuition as reasoning from the

heart—direct knowledge from our feeling self, without any input or distortion from our thinking mind.

Tara has a really good sense of intuition. I remember her calling me from a play date when she was in second grade. She said she had a stomachache, and when I went to pick her up, I realized that she was uncomfortable at the house. She felt unsafe around the boys who were there playing with her friend's siblings. I told Tara that day to always trust what her body is telling her, and she has developed an uncanny sense of judgment not just for herself, but for other people. Recently my father had an overzealous business associate who had charmed all of us. Tara repeatedly told me that she didn't like the man, and I would tell her to be polite. As it turned out, the guy was a fake and a cheat, and put my father in a precarious situation. Tara was right all along.

My own experience has taught me the power of trusting intuition. Following its whispers, though it's often difficult, has never led me astray. In 1995, I was working at MTV, and the company needed someone to coordinate its efforts in India. My managers agreed that I was a good fit for the job, given my familiarity with MTV strategy and my family connections there. So at twenty-three I moved to my family's homeland. It was thrilling to be in India during a time when the market was opening up to international partners, and I felt blessed to have the opportunity to help unite the world through music. I could not have asked for a better position from which to shape my career. Not only was my job at the crossroads of brand building, marketing, programming, and production, but it also required me to socialize with expats from around the world. My business card could get me into any club or restaurant. It was a dream job for a young person.

I happily threw myself into the work, but within a week or so of arriving I developed an odd symptom: I started getting stomachaches, especially in the morning. I chalked it up to the food or maybe a little homesickness or the pressure to be successful—or a combination of all three—and tried to ignore it as best I could. But the discomfort persisted.

Finally, one day my team had a huge breakthrough. We sold our first sponsorship package to a multinational company. It was a big win, and my coworkers and I celebrated, clinking champagne glasses in our air-conditioned car as we drove through the streets of Mumbai. At one point during the drive we found ourselves stuck in a traffic jam—not an unusual occurrence in India. Looking ahead, we saw that a crowd of children, shoeless and in tattered clothing, was blocking the road. As we drew closer, we realized that they were gathered around a makeshift roadside stall, watching television. The tiny TV hung precariously from wires jerry-rigged to the stall's side. On the screen was a beach scene. Teenagers dressed in skimpy bikinis and shorts were grinding and gyrating to hip-hop music. In the top corner of the screen was the MTV logo.

My coworkers cheered, high-fived each other, and poured more champagne. These kids were watching our channel. Here was proof of how successfully we were penetrating the market! But my heart stopped in that moment. I literally did not breathe. Instead of joy, I felt a creeping sense of shame.

I went home early that night, long before the endless celebrating was over, but I couldn't sleep. As I lay in bed, the questions started swirling: *What am I doing? Is this the effect I want to have on the world?* I had wanted to unite it through music, not export the superficial aspects of American culture to my family's homeland. I loved my job, but in that moment I knew that this career wasn't aligned with my life's purpose. A part of me wanted to ignore the voice that told me I was on the wrong path, wanted to continue doing what I was doing. It was fun, and I was good at it, but the voice grew louder as the weeks went by, and eventually I knew I had to make a change. I had to trust that quiet inner voice. The day I finally acknowledged that I needed to quit my job was the day my stomachaches went away.

Intuition often comes from the body, as it did with my stomach pains in India. It can warn us we're not on the right path, alert us to trouble—and even guide us toward healthy choices. My body, for a few years now, was telling me it was time to unravel why I was making unhealthy choices with food when I knew better. There is no question that choosing healthy foods makes us feel more energetic, while eating sugar and junk can leave us sluggish and moody. So why do I keep making those choices? I could use some help there. Until now, I've been reluctant to examine my complicated relationship with food. But if my intent is to treat my body considerately, I need to unpack this tricky issue. My dad's book *What Are You Hungry For?* is among those stacked by my bedside. One morning after I take the girls to school, I think, *It's time*. So I head upstairs and grab the book.

I open it randomly, something I've always liked to do, just to see what my eyes will fall on first. It's actually an ancient practice known as bibliomancy, a kind of divination that's supposed to offer insight and wisdom. It doesn't always work, but more often than not I'm amazed at the information that comes to me in this manner. In any case, when I open my dad's book, my eyes light upon these words: "If you trust your body to know what you need, it will take care of you." The body knows when it's hungry and full because the gut sends hormonal signals to the brain, my dad explains. You just need to pay attention—and trust your body's messages.

> You just need to pay attention—and trust your body's messages.

Trust your body. In all my many diets and dozens of

attempts to curtail a sugar habit, I have ignored this simple advice. It's such an obvious idea, and yet it has never been part of my weight-loss strategy. My body is designed, as everyone's is, to be in balance and maintain a certain weight. But because of my emotional attachment to food, I've been systematically overriding its signals that tell me I'm full, and eating when I'm not really hungry.

To learn to trust my body, I need to tune in to its signals, so I decide to follow a simple approach my father outlines. Before eating, he suggests, practice STOP, for *Stop* what you're doing; *Take* a one-minute breathing break, inhaling and exhaling and paying attention to the breath; *Observe* your hunger, rating it on a scale of one to five, with five being famished; then *Proceed* with awareness.

It's incredibly similar to an idea Daniel Siegel told me about called response flexibility—to pause before responding so you can become aware of what's happening in the moment and consider your options. "Pausing helps you make wise choices," Siegel had told me. If ever I need to make wise choices, it's when I'm faced with a bakery full of cupcakes.

I close the book for a moment, struck by the fact that the issue of trust, which I consider central to fulfilling intentions, is also a key part of learning to eat in a way that will help maintain a healthy weight. And I can do it without dieting because tuning in to my body's hunger and fullness cues should help me eat what I need, but no more.

The most enduring and challenging part of my diet is the sugar habit. If anything makes me feel like a failure, it's my inability to conquer this problem. When I was a young girl, my father tried to hypnotize me out of my craving for sweets. He had me envision slimy green frogs covered in chocolate and bring them up to my mouth. I wanted to gag from the visualization. It actually worked for a day or two, but then I was back at it. My love of chocolate was strong enough to overcome revulsion. Since then I've been on and off the sugar wagon more times than I can count.

Why is it so difficult to change this habit for good? For one thing, there's evidence that sugar has addictive qualities. Some research shows it hits the same pleasure centers in the brain as heroin. I do a little research on habit formation and learn that changing entrenched habits is far harder than I thought. The best study on the topic was published in 2010 by researchers at University College in London. They recruited ninety-six volunteers and asked each of them to choose one behavior or activity they wanted to add to their lives. The median length of time that elapsed before participants hit the habit plateau was 66 days—more than three times longer than the widely reported myth of 21 days—but there was a surprisingly wide range, from 18 to 254 days. Although missing a day here and there didn't seem to matter much in terms of the overall ability to form the habit, the people who were most consistent were also the most likely to be successful. But certain types of behaviors took longer to adopt, regardless of commitment.

Eating-related practices took sixty-five days, on average, while exercise-related activities didn't become automatic until participants had been doing them routinely for roughly ninety days. The researchers speculate that getting in the habit of physical activity takes longer because it's more complicated than eating more vegetables or drinking more water, and as a result, requires more mental effort. Motivation undoubtedly matters too, but even if you're motivated, it's not easy. In this study, in which participants really wanted to make a change, about *half* didn't perform the behavior consistently enough to transform it into a habit.

Although the research is a little depressing, it also helps me to see that slipups and failures are a normal part of the process—and that helps me realize that I need to be forgiving with myself when I backslide and simply reaffirm my intents. The reality is I haven't ever gone for more than one, maybe two weeks without sugar.

I fell in love with the sweet stuff as a kid. My grandmother loves chocolate as much as I do, and some of my fondest memories from our visits to India are of playing in Nani's house while she made a chocolate cake or whipped together delicious milkshakes. Even now, imagining those days fills me with a warm, cozy feeling, and I suddenly see part of the problem. In my mind, sugar means security, protection, safety. It's a refuge, a haven. No wonder I reach for sweet treats to soothe myself when I'm sad or anxious, scared or uncertain. It's not just that it tastes good; it tastes like love.

In my father's book, he says the task of people struggling with weight and food is this: *find your fulfillment*. Food alone can't fulfill you, my dad writes. "You must nourish the body with healthy food, the heart with joy, compassion and love, the mind with knowledge and the spirit with equanimity and self-awareness. . . . If you fill yourself with other kinds of satisfaction, food will no longer be a problem." Those words strike home. Isn't that what I'm trying to do this year—to find the many nonedible things that fill me up?

I let this idea settle into my soul. Instead of finding satisfaction from a variety of sources, I've become overreliant on food, turning to it not just for physical nourishment but also for emotional sustenance. Which means I need to focus on the other things in my life that provide joy, compassion, and love. An inveterate list maker, I jot down some quick ideas under the heading "Ways to Find Fulfillment Without Food."

Talk to people I love. Take my girls to the beach. Go for a walk. Do a puzzle. Read a novel. Serve food to others.

All things that dovetail with my most heartfelt intents—bringing more joy to my life, connecting with family and friends, relaxing and giving back to my community. If I can trust that I can find love and fulfillment from sources other than chocolate chip cookies and ice cream, then that is a first step. It will take patience and habit breaking, but if I start adding activities that feed me in deeper ways, I know I can find the right balance.

As the days go by, before I eat anything, I ask myself: What are you hungry for? I'm stunned at the number of times the answer isn't in the refrigerator. Sometimes I'm restless, and a walk around the block cures my craving. Sometimes I'm thirsty and a big glass of water hits the spot. One day when I'm dying for a chocolate chip cookie, I realize what I'm really longing for is connection. Because reestablishing contact with old friends is one of my intents, it's a win-win.

I pick up the phone and call one of my closest friends, Sayantani. Like me, Sayantani has two kids, and she balances being a mom with writing and a medical career. "It's been a while," she says when she hears my voice. I apologize, feeling a sharp spike of guilt. I need to be better about staying in touch. As we chat, I tell her about my intent to eat healthier and trust my body. "You need to read about intuitive eating," she says. "It's all about trusting your body. And there's research showing it works."

I go online and find tons of information. The philosophy is simple: Eat when you're hungry, stop when you're full. And eat what your body is telling you it wants. If a milkshake is really, honestly what I need, I should have it. The concept is liberating.

I start paying more attention to what I really want to eat as well as how the food makes me feel as I eat it. As I learn to trust my body, I notice that when it comes to sweets, I'm often satisfied after a few bites, especially if I eat mindfully, enjoying the smell and sight of the food and chewing slowly so I can savor the moment. One day, I have a few bites of a chocolate bar, relishing each bite. And by the time I'm halfway through, my body sends a startling message: *You've had enough.* I think about it for a minute and realize it's true. My enjoyment is starting to diminish, and a sickly feeling is starting to kick in. So I store the second half in the fridge for later.

Did that just happen? I think jubilantly.

I also try to eat more mindfully at every meal. Instead of diving into my food the second I sit down, I enjoy the look of my meal—the colors, the textures. I smell it, savoring the aroma. I feel grateful to the farmers who grew it and the people who transported it to the store. I have a sip of water. Once I'm eating, I try to really taste everything—the sweet, the salty, the pungent, the bitter. I chew at least ten times before swallowing. And before the next bite, I pause and notice how my body feels. Am I full? Do I need more? What is my body telling me? Trusting and noticing, two steps of the intent process, are now working in harmony, seamlessly and beautifully.

As I practice this way of eating, it becomes more automatic over time, and I start to see that my body really does send plenty of messages about my level of hunger, especially when I eat more slowly. Research shows it takes twenty minutes for the gut to register that it's full and send that message to the brain; if I gobble my food, I don't give this innate signaling system time to do its job. Another reminder that I need to trust my body.

One afternoon when I'm midway through a cupcake, it hits me that I'm not supposed to be eating it. *You deserve it*, I tell myself. *It's been a stressful day*. But that tried-and-true assurance rings hollow. *What are you doing?* I ask myself. The answer is discouraging: the same thing I always do when I'm stressed, having a sugary snack. I tell myself I want to change, that I want to eat more healthfully, but this habit is so hard to break! Sugar is terrible for me. I know this. Already I can feel the semisickening rush as those sweet molecules hit my bloodstream; for maybe a half hour I'll have a happy buzz. And I can predict with utter certainty what will happen next: I'll be tired and cranky and my brain will feel as if it's stuffed with cotton candy. Spun sugar. How appropriate.

I'm angry and frustrated—and filled with self-loathing. *I'm hopeless. I'll never get this right!* My mind continues along that unpleasant track for some time. *No wonder I weigh too much. Why am I so weak?* Thanks to my noticing practice, I catch myself midtirade.

Stop, I think. *That's not nice. Nobody deserves that kind of treatment.* And as soon as those kind words cross my mind, I'm flooded with a feeling of tenderness—for myself and my struggle, and for the millions of other people who fight this same battle with food. *You're trying,* I tell myself. *It's OK.*

I remember when Tara and Leela were learning to walk. They'd take single, wobbly steps, then fall. I didn't get angry with them. I cheered their attempts and encouraged their effort. I accepted their falls and failures as part of the process. I saw every wobble, lurch, and plop as heartwarming and humorous

> I didn't get angry with them. I cheered their attempts and encouraged their effort. I accepted their falls and failures as part of the process.

rather than as cause for despair. Working with intent should be no different; it's a process—one we should approach seriously but lightly, with a sense of curiosity, exploration, eagerness, and hope, and as little self-recrimination as possible.

Trusting yourself requires a hefty measure of self-compassion—and as it turns out, so does learning to eat healthfully or changing any habit. More and more research is showing that treating ourselves with compassion, just as we would a cherished friend, actually helps us adopt healthy habits.

For instance, researchers from Duke University found that people who are gentle and understanding in their self-talk, who forgive themselves when they slip up, and who recognize that everyone goes through periods of ups and downs are more likely to incorporate healthy practices into their lives, such as visiting their doctors and practicing safe sex. Likewise, Canadian researchers found that women who scored higher on a self-compassion scale were more likely to exercise because it's good for them rather than because it made them look good—and those who work out for health reasons are more likely to stick with it. And a study in Portugal found that overweight women who were participating in a year-long weight-loss program became more religious about eating healthfully after they were taught to be more accepting of their bodies.

Beating myself up isn't just painful, it's counterproductive. So this is yet another jagged piece of the living-with-intent puzzle. As I continue forward in this project, I'm going to try to do so with a sense of self-compassion. As the Roman Catholic saint Francis de Sales advocated, I'll carry with me "a cup of understanding, a barrel of love and an ocean of patience." It's that, or a tsunami of self-recrimination. Why not choose love?

Choose self-love and self-compassion, trusting that it takes time and patience to make hard changes. We all have our mountains to climb and hurdles to overcome. We need to support our own efforts, just as we offer support to family and friends—and trust that when we ask for help from those we love, they will offer it up with open arms and warm embraces.

As I continue to think about my relationship to food, diet, and health, and how to get those things on track in my life, I receive a voice mail from Dr. Andrew Weil, director of the Center for Integrative Medicine at the University of Arizona. For a month or so I've been trying to set up an interview with him. I admire how he, along with my father, has helped change the conversation in the medical establishment about what it means to be healthy. Turns out Dr. Weil will be speaking at an event at the Chopra Center in La Costa this weekend. *Can you meet me there?* he asks on my voice mail. I immediately call his assistant and confirm that yes, thank you, I will see him. The timing is perfect, given the food issues I've been dealing with. Thank you, universe! Even my girls are excited about this interview. Weil is a cofounder of True Foods restaurants, a family favorite and the place Leela, a picky eater, first tried (and fell in love with) pizza.

When I arrive at the Center, the receptionists smile and welcome me. The staff at the Chopra Center are the warmest, gentlest, and most dedicated people I have met. I tell them that I am expecting Dr. Weil and will wait for him in David Simon's old office. *Oh, David,* I think sadly. Even the mention of his name makes my heart ache, but also swell with love and fond memories. He cofounded the Chopra Center with my father, and he was my dad's partner in figuring out ways to help people integrate mind/body practices into their everyday routines. David was a close friend of mine as well, and as I sit in his old office waiting for Dr. Weil, I think about him and the inspiring work he did here. David died in January 2012 after diagnosing himself with a glioblastoma brain tumor twenty months earlier. His passing left a vast hole not only in his own family but also at the Chopra Center and in all of us who loved him.

Just as I'm starting to feel really blue, my father walks into the room, bringing with him a refreshing burst of energy and enthusiasm. He's just been on the phone with scientists from Harvard and the National Institutes of Health, and he's excited; they're exploring a research study on the benefits of integrating wellness principles into healthy aging programs. He looks at David's photo and bows slightly. The gesture brings tears to my eyes. It's so lovely—and reassuring. Although David is no longer physically here, my father clearly feels his presence keenly—and wants David to know that he's carrying on their work and that they are still making progress together.

Dr. Weil walks in, dressed in jeans and a plaid shirt. He greets us warmly, and he and my dad catch up briefly. I smile as I listen in. They're both delighted that so many people are attending this weekend's seminar. It reminds me of one of the things I've always admired about my father: he doesn't take his fame for granted. In fact, he's still amazed and thrilled that his work has resonated with so many people around the world.

As Weil and I sit down to talk, I explain my book and the idea of intent. "I believe the universe responds to your intent," he agrees enthusiastically. "But a large part of that is trust. You need to trust that you can do what it is you set out to do, and even if you're not getting external validation, you need to trust the universe to support you."

The idea of trusting your intentions, he says, reminds him of something that happened to him a while back—an incident that was so meaningful to him he's including the story in a book he's writing about his life. He tells me his story:

I lived on a ranch outside of Tucson on a rural property. It was truly in the wilderness. One spring day a man who took care of the property came to me and said he'd found a baby owl and didn't know what to do about it. So I followed him out to a part of the property where these huge cottonwood trees were growing. And there on the ground was this tiny owl, only a few inches high, covered in whitish fluff. It was hopping around, peeping, clearly in distress. I looked up, and way above us on one of the cottonwood branches—it must have been thirty feet high—I saw a huge nest. And peering down at us from the nest was a great horned owl. I knew it had to be the baby's mother.

Either the baby had fallen or been pushed out of the nest. Either way, I had no idea what to do about it, but I figured feeding it would be a good place to start. The little thing must be hungry, right? So I got some wet dog food, but the owl wouldn't eat it. Then I put some sugar water in a dropper, and it drank a little. I felt good about that. What I really needed was a long-term solution, so I called the zoology department at the University of Arizona. Nobody answered, so I called the Desert Museum, an indoor/outdoor nature preserve. They said they'd find someone who would know what to do.

A few minutes later my phone rang. On the other end was this old guy. No idea who he was. He didn't even give his name. He just said, "You have to put the baby back in the nest." I was taken aback. The nest was way high up in the cottonwood tree, and the mother was in the nest. Great

*horned owls have been known to attack people, especially
when they feel threatened. "Isn't that dangerous?" I asked.*

*"She will know what you are doing," he said. And he
hung up.*

*So I asked the man who had found the owl to get the
tallest ladder he could find. By this time I was getting pretty
anxious. I don't like heights, and just looking up at the nest
made me feel a little queasy. But what choice did I have?
We secured the ladder as best we could against the tree, and
I picked up the chick and started to climb. From the moment
I started up the ladder, the mother owl locked eyes with me,
and the whole time I climbed we didn't break eye contact.
She didn't move a muscle, and her eyes didn't waver. It felt
as if I were climbing forever, but I finally got up to the nest.
There was a dead rattlesnake hanging out of it. It was very
dramatic. I'm surprised I didn't fall off the ladder from the
shock of that sight. I reached over, placed the chick slowly in
the nest, and climbed back down. Later that day, another
man who was working on the property walked past that
tree, and the mother owl dove out of the nest toward him,
screeching, with her talons exposed. I realized that the old
guy was right: The mother owl knew exactly what I was
doing. She had read my intentions and trusted me. And I
had trusted her.*

As I'm driving home after the interview, I think about
his story and realize we all have an inner owl—watchful,

worried, ready to strike out of fear but also capable of trust. When we feel threatened, we lash out. But when we trust the universe, things often work out for the best. We get our babies back into the nest, we launch them safely into the world—maybe we even learn to feed ourselves healthy food and take better care of our bodies. We move closer and closer to fulfilling our intent.

INTENTIONAL LIVING:
REFLECTIONS AND PRACTICES

Trust is an important step in realizing your intentions: trusting yourself—your desires, your intuitions, and your ability to succeed—as well as trusting the universe, that the people, places, and circumstances presented to you are part of the journey.

1. Before eating your next snack or meal, take a moment and ask yourself, "What am I hungry for?" Trust the answers that come from both your mind and your body.

2. When you are next in a stressful situation, STOP. Stop, Take three breaths, Observe how you are feeling, and then Proceed. Trust your feelings—in your body as well as your mind.

3. Dreams can sometimes give you insight into your subconscious desires. Keep a dream journal. For one week, every morning before you get out of bed, take a moment to record any dreams you remember. It may be that you just note colors you saw or feelings you had. Write

down everything, and when the week ends, contemplate the connections and feelings these dreams bring up. Your dreams may be sending you messages about how to achieve your intentions.

INTENT PRACTICE: TRUSTING
YOUR BODY'S MESSAGES

One way to tune in to what your body is feeling is with a body-scan practice. I try to do it at least once a week. It's a great way to learn to trust what your body is telling you.

- Find a comfortable place to lie down. Close your eyes. Take a few deep breaths and notice how your chest expands and contracts with each breath. Pay attention to the nurturing aspect of breath: how each inhale brings in oxygen to nurture your body, how with each exhale you release stress and toxins.

- As you continue to breathe, shift your attention to the crown of your head. Feel any tension you're holding there and try to release it. Bring your attention to the action of your brain. Feel a moment of gratitude for the awesomeness of the human brain—for all those neurons regulating every aspect of your physical existence. Notice any sensation in your head that's uncomfortable. If there is discomfort, direct your next several breaths to that place. Do not judge or fear the pain, just notice how it makes you feel and whether the breathing helps.

- Move your attention to your neck and shoulders. Again, breathe deeply and notice any tension in these areas. Imagine your breath is opening up the knots in your neck or releasing tension from your shoulders.

- Move down your left arm to your left hand, breathing deeply as you notice the joints in your elbows and wrists and through the tips of your fingers. Do the same for your right arm and hand.

- Continue the practice, working your way through the rest of your body—your heart, lungs, stomach and organs, your pelvis, legs, and feet. Appreciate what each does for you as you continue to breathe.

- For the next few minutes, shift your attention back to your breath. You may notice that your mind is drawn to the part of your body that feels uncomfortable. Trust the message this sends you: that this is the area where you're holding tension or that requires extra loving care.

- Be present and enjoy this moment of honoring your body, checking in and taking care of yourself.

FIVE

EXPRESS

It's New Year's Day, and we're in Vietnam, visiting my brother-in-law, Hemant, and his family, who have been living in Hanoi for the past year. Hemant works for the International Finance Corporation, a part of the United Nations World Bank that invests in development projects, and we've been keen to visit while they're living in Southeast Asia. What an opportunity for introducing the girls to a different culture! Just as important, my girls have been eager to spend time with their two-and-a-half-year-old cousin Tahira, as well as their aunt, uncle, and grandparents. My in-laws have joined us from India so that we can be together over the girls' winter vacation.

After a breakfast of fresh-baked croissants, fruit, prosciutto, and cheese from the local French Vietnamese bakery, Tara, Leela, Sumant, and I get dressed and head out to see some of the sights in Hanoi. Our first stop is the

Vietnam Military History Museum, where we get a glimpse into the Vietnam War from the Vietnamese perspective—namely, that they successfully repelled a prolonged attack by the French and Americans.

The girls haven't yet studied the Vietnam War in school, so Sumant and I explain briefly what it was about. We tell them about the fear of communism and how the anti-Communist message was, for many years, the central focus of U.S. foreign policy and the driving force behind a number of wars and escalating international tension and conflict.

We stroll past an array of downed U.S. military planes, helicopters, and tanks; and in the courtyard we stop to look at a graphic sculpture meant to signify Vietnam's victory. It's an American B-52, nose down, as if it crashed there, surrounded by scrap metal; an evocative photo of a woman dragging the wreckage of a plane sits in front of the sculpture.

Tara and Leela are quiet as we look at the piece. They're not sheltered exactly, but they're still young, and I can tell they're trying to assimilate this new information about the violence of war with what they know of the world so far. It's not easy, even for adults. We spend so much time trying to teach our children to respect other people's points of view. How do you explain that differences of opinion can lead to so many lost lives? At what point is it right to die for your beliefs? Is killing for them ever justified?

In a sense, war is a country's or culture's most extreme

way of expressing an intent. Horrifying as it is, at its heart war is a desire to defend—and express—a deeply held point of view, whether it's a belief in communism or democracy or a particular religion.

As we wander among the planes and bombs at the war museum, Tara is particularly quiet, and I wonder if all the scenes of suffering have been too much for her. But when she asks, "Can people have bad intents?" I see that she's actually thinking deeply about the things we've seen. Her question is one I get asked a lot. Although my goal—and the goal of most people—is to use intent for good, for bringing more compassion, love, and understanding into the world, there are people who merely want to impose their beliefs on everyone else.

"Absolutely, intents can be used for evil purposes," I tell Tara. We talk about Hitler, whose despicable intent was embraced by a generation of Germans, and even how Senator Joseph McCarthy's intent to protect the world from communism fueled paranoia and suspicion in the United States, pitting friends and colleagues against one another. I'm glad we're discussing this aspect of intent, because it's been on my mind as I've dived deeper into this project.

"And many intents aren't necessarily evil, but they're driven by the ego rather than by a desire to bring good into the world," I tell the girls. I remind them of our visit several days before to Angkor Wat in Siem Reap, Cambodia. Angkor Wat is the largest religious building in the world, and as we strolled the grounds, I found myself bowled over by its lessons about intent. The structure is an imposing and impressive tribute to the Hindu god Vishnu—and the will of the Khmer king Suryavarman II, who reigned from 1113 to 1150. Like other monarchs in ancient times, King Suryavarman had a vision to create a monument to his own power and dominance. Gazing at the massive structure, I remember Eckhart Tolle distinguishing between egoic, or ego-based, intents and nonegoic intents during our conversation. Egoic intents are ones that feed the ego, while nonegoic intents serve the greater good. Angkor Wat is something of a combination of each, inspired by spiritual fervor as well as the king's grandiose ideas of his own self-importance.

Now, as I talk to my girls about evil and ego-driven intents, I realize that all intents share an important unifying thread: they gain strength through the power of expression. Hitler swayed the Nazi Party with the intensity of his rhetoric. Angkor Wat rose from the ground, stone by stone, because the king decreed it. Vietnam and the United States were determined to express and defend their own perspectives, even if it meant killing and dying for them.

> All intents share an important unifying thread: they gain strength through the power of expression.

Fortunately, I tell the girls, by expressing wise intents

you also have the power to change the world. "Think about Martin Luther King Jr. and his 'I Have a Dream' speech or John Kennedy vowing to put the first man on the moon," I say. "Putting desires into words and expressing your deepest dreams can help transform them into reality—and change the world for the better."

The distinction between good and evil or ego-based intentions is an important one for me as I move forward in this project, because it figures heavily into the idea of expressing intents. Expressing an intention is the first baby step toward taking action, and as a result, it's the stage at which an intent is most likely to start affecting other people. If your intent is to make the world a better place, you need to make sure your words and actions reflect that deeper value.

> If your intent is to make the world a better place, you need to make sure your words and actions reflect that deeper value.

At its simplest, expressing an intent is just what it sounds like. It's expressing your deepest dreams. But there are many different ways you can do it. You can write down your intent, repeat it in your mind, say it aloud, share it with a close friend or family member, or put it out into the wider world, on the Internet, in a newspaper article—even in a book. I created Intent.com in part to give people a place to express their intents, because I firmly believe that by expressing our most heartfelt aims, whether in writing or verbally, silently or aloud, we crystallize the thought behind the ideas and mobilize the energy to make them happen. We take ownership of the desire and make it our own, and we actively solicit other people, seek opportunities, and embrace faith to support our vision.

In the Hindu tradition, we don't explicitly say wedding vows as is done in Western traditions. Our weddings involve walking around a fire seven times, symbolically representing vows we make to each other and our families. But I've attended many Western weddings (Christian and Jewish) over the years, and I'm always struck by how the ceremonies are among the loveliest and most deeply moving expressions of intention. When you stand up in front of your closest family and friends and vow to be faithful to one person for the rest of your life, you're not only validating your relationship, you're also embracing a set of values: love, loyalty, commitment. It's a way of saying to yourself and the world: I believe in love. Ultimately, the desire for love—whether self-love or love for others—lies at the heart of most intents. The need for love is as basic and fundamental as the need for oxygen and water, and like those two

> Love motivates us to be our best and do our best for the world, which is what living with intent is all about.

necessary elements, we can't function without it. Love motivates us to be our best and do our best for the world, which is what living with intent is all about.

Because the truest intents often center on love, "expressing" your intent isn't always about saying things. You can also show love and act with love. I express my intent to love my daughters when I prepare them food, listen to their worries, guide their choices, provide a safe, happy home. I express my love for Sumant by picking up his clothes from the dry cleaner, supporting him in his work projects, listening to him as he decompresses from a stressful day. I express love for myself when I sit down to meditate, when I eat a healthy meal, when I take the time to call my mother because I need some reassuring words. Whether we're seeking love or trying to live each day with love guiding the way, expressing plays a role in the process.

The day comes that we need to leave Vietnam and return home, and the girls are sad to say good-bye to their cousin, aunt, uncle, and grandparents. So I sit them down and say, "We still have a few hours left. Do you want to spend it feeling sad, or shall we express an intent to enjoy our time with our family while we're here?"

"Will that help?" Leela asks, brown eyes shining with fresh tears.

"Definitely," I promise. And I believe it. By saying the words aloud you can make their content a reality.

The girls look at me solemnly, tears in their big eyes, and say, "My intent is to have fun with Tahira." We take a moment to appreciate the intent, and then they are off and giggling. They spend the rest of the time before we leave for the airport happily playing with their sweet cousin and cuddling with their grandparents.

I've come to think of these miniwishes as microintents, and I'm struck again by how expressing them clearly can help set the tone for a day and consciously shape my experience and outlook. On Intent.com, a number of users share daily intents to focus on positive thoughts or to do one sun salutation every day for a week, and they often report that it helps them change the shape of their days.

> Microintents may seem so small as to be meaningless, but I've learned that there's enormous power in baby steps.

Microintents may seem so small as to be meaningless, but I've learned that there's enormous power in baby steps. They have a profound effect not only in the short term—making our day-to-day lives healthier and happier—but they can also set the stage for, and help us move toward, our long-term intentions. Articulating them clearly and frequently gives them more power.

For instance, one day I knew I was going to face some

stress and chaos at work. A potential investor in Intent.com had backed out of supporting the company after months of conversations. I had to explain to my other investors what had happened, as well as come up with a new budget and plan for the company because we would not be receiving money we were all counting on. I was stressed, disappointed, anxious, and angry. But I knew that those emotions would not help me get through the day. So to arm myself, I meditated before making those first phone calls. I set a clear intent, posting it on Intent.com: *My intent is to remain centered in the midst of chaos.* I felt that by expressing it clearly—not just to myself but also to our subscribers—I'd give my intent greater potency.

Immediately I received a number of supportive responses on the site, all of which boosted my confidence and gave me the sense that I could get through this challenging time. As the day progressed and the angry reactions from my other investors came pouring in via e-mail and voice mail, I silently expressed my intent, reaffirming the desire to remain calm. Every time I reminded myself, I took a few deep breaths, giving my body and mind a chance to settle into stillness for a moment. When I wavered from that place of calmness to panic, which happened throughout that day, I'd notice what was happening—my racing heart, my sweating palms—and I would think back to the morning and my intent. Those eleven words served as an anchor for the entire day. Despite the pandemonium and upset swirling around me, I felt like the eye of the storm, a point of stillness and quiet in the center of the tumult. It was a remarkably powerful sensation.

Rather than being swept away, I was able to make reasonable judgments, provide support and guidance, and maintain my equanimity. I reassured our investors and supporters that I believed in the company, and I promised that we would come up with alternative funding sources. I think my example helped keep some of the intensity in check. The calm of that single day didn't change my life, but it changed that day, turning what could have been a miserable ten hours into something that felt manageable. In the scheme of things, I count that not as a microachievement but rather as a big success.

Working with microintents is a great way to dip your toe into the intent process. Are there microintents that can help you get through a difficult day? Affirmations help anchor and center us; they also remind us of what's important and why we make certain choices in our lives. You may be surprised by how much peace—even joy—you can find on the most difficult days by anchoring them with heartfelt intentions.

It was actually my friend Lisa who first got me thinking about the power of expressing daily microintents. She decided to set an intent every day for a week. Before heading to her stressful job at a magazine, she would take a few minutes to write a daily intent in her journal. *My intent is to come up with a new idea today. My intent is to tune in to my inner voice rather than reacting. My intent is to connect with one of my coworkers in a genuine way.* After the first week she noticed that her microintents seemed related to larger themes of creativity and connecting to others in new ways.

Lisa spent her day managing others or embroiled in meetings, then rushing to after-work events. Because she was so busy, she struggled to find the time to access the creativity and connection she craved, and each evening she noticed that she had not manifested her microintent. But instead of feeling disappointed, she saw this new information as evidence that she needed to make a change. She wasn't living in a way that was aligned with her deeper values or emotional needs. In other words, she approached the experience with an open, curious mind instead of an attitude of judgment, and as a result gained important insight into what was missing from her life. This led her organically to a period of incubation, during which she vowed to think about and work toward her larger intent. Did she need to change careers, or was there a way to shape her current job into something that better suited her needs?

One year later, Lisa was celebrating her fiftieth birthday. Instead of having a big party, she celebrated by inviting her closest friends to participate in an evening of expressing what they wanted in the next phase of their lives. "It was a night of sharing dreams," she says. At the gathering Lisa shared an intent that had been incubating for some time: She wanted to take her yoga practice to another level by attending a month-long retreat. It seemed like such an outlandish fantasy that she was afraid to even acknowledge she wanted to do it. And she was reluctant to ask her family and colleagues for the support she'd need to pull it off. She'd have to recalibrate her busy work schedule as well as her family life with her husband and two kids. Even so, for the first time, in the safe circle of her dear friends, she expressed her intent out loud—and everyone encouraged her to make it a reality. In that moment, she set the wheels in motion to commit to the retreat. She mustered the courage to bring it up with her sons and boss, and they all were surprisingly supportive. Her sons were actually excited about spending a month alone with her husband and doing "guy stuff." And her work associates were impressed and even a little envious of her courage to express what she wanted—and make it happen.

Lisa took responsibility for where she was in her life and found support—but she might not have gotten there if she hadn't expressed her dreams to others.

Lisa's story reminds me that it can be challenging to express an intent, and here's why: it often involves asking someone else to do something on your behalf—to share your burden, to listen to what you say, to give you time or space, or even money. For women, who seem almost biologically programmed to help everyone else but are loath to ask for anything for themselves, one of the biggest sticking points in fulfilling intents is the inability to express what we want. Maybe it's because we think we don't deserve it, or because we believe that asking for things is selfish or self-centered. Either way, the inability to express our want is a stumbling block that comes up time and again on the road to intent, one we must surmount if we want to actually live the life we envision.

I've bumped up against the problem a number of times. Over the years, I've started several companies, and each time I've had to approach potential investors. I find it incredibly hard each time, and I can't say it has become any easier. While I've always believed strongly in my vision for the company, it has been difficult for me to ask other people to buy into it. Bringing others on board is a huge responsibility. I'm accountable for what happens. But it's also asking other people to believe in me and my dreams. It's telling myself and the world that my life, my ideas, my vision are valuable and worthy of commitment and effort. And that's scary. I've forced myself to have those uncomfortable meetings with potential investors by asking myself these questions: Do I have faith that what I'm

> Do I have faith that what I'm creating will be good not just for me but for many others as well? Will it serve a deeper purpose?

creating will be good not just for me but for many others as well? Will it serve a deeper purpose?

Those questions can help all of us when we're struggling to ask others for support. When the answer to such questions is yes, let that knowledge guide you and give you the confidence to move forward, to say what you want out loud, and do what you have to do to realize your dreams.

The belief in expressing our desires runs deeply through the heart of many of the world's religions. Mark 11:24 says: *Therefore I tell you, whatever you ask in prayer, believe that you have received it, and it will be yours.* And Matthew 7:7–8: *Ask, and it will be given to you; seek, and you will find; knock, and it will be opened to you. For every one who asks receives, and he who seeks finds, and to him who knocks it will be opened.*

It's the basis of *metta,* or loving-kindness, meditation too. Meant to develop the four qualities of love—friendliness, compassion, appreciative joy, and equanimity—the heartfelt practice includes repeating phrases throughout the meditation, starting with something like this: *May I be well. May I be happy. May I be at ease. May I be peaceful.* After several minutes of wishing yourself these qualities, you expand the wish to your family, your friends, the people you pass on the street—*May you be well. May you be happy*—and then the whole of humankind. *May all beings be well. May all beings be happy.*

Expressing intents is deeply embedded in Shintoism as well—a practice my family and I experienced firsthand on a trip to Japan in 2008. Our first tourist destination was the Meiji Jingu, a Shinto shrine that sits in the lovely Yoyogi Park, near Tokyo's Harajuku district. The temple is a haven of peace and serenity, and the walk to the main shrine took us through woods filled with thousands of cypress trees, gifted by people from all over the country after the death of Emperor Meiji and Empress Shoken in 1912 and 1914, respectively.

In the inner shrine, we came upon row after row of small wood panels, called *ema*, hanging from hooks, clicking gently together with each small gust of wind. The panels had drawings and handwriting on them, and we learned that visitors are meant to write their wishes on the wooden plaques. We stood there for several moments, moved by the sight of hundreds of *ema* left by individual visitors. When we looked closer, we saw that on each one were private wishes—for world peace, family harmony, health, love, compassion, forgiveness, tolerance. It brought to mind the practice in Jerusalem of writing a prayer on a scrap of paper and placing it in a crack in the Western Wall, a Jewish holy site in the Old City. More than a million people place notes in the wall each year, and they're collected twice a year and buried on the nearby Mount of Olives.

I've always loved the idea of writing down intents and leaving them somewhere, as if handing them over to the universe. So as our extended family wandered around the temple grounds, I bought *ema* panels for Tara, Leela, and myself. We took our time composing our thoughts and writing our wishes. I wished for health and happiness for my family—my single most important wish, then and always.

As we hung our *ema* on hooks, we were told that at the end of the month, the resident monks would collect the panels, contemplate the messages, then burn them. I imagined our dreams drifting out into the waiting arms of the universe, and the notion filled me with a sense of peace.

Expressing an intent by writing it on an *ema* is a graphic way of soliciting the universe for help, but the reality is, every time you express an intent you are turning to the universe (or God or the divine). And I've seen it work in profoundly moving ways.

My friend Arielle Ford, a personal-growth expert and author, changed her life when she began expressing her intent to meet her soul mate. I sit down with her for tea one lovely winter day at my parents' house to hear the story.

At the age of forty-four, after many rich relationships that ended for one reason or another, Arielle badly wanted to meet the man she was supposed to be with for the rest of her life. And she believed he was out there looking for her too. She envisioned what she wanted in a partner and made a "soul mate" list that identified the qualities she sought, then she started living her life as if he would be there soon.

She also visualized him with her whole being. "I tried to feel the visualization in my body—really feel that what I'd asked for was already mine, in the present moment," she says. Each day at sunset, she lit candles and sat in a comfy chair. She closed her eyes and imagined the joy of being with her soul mate, and the all-encompassing love she would feel. She allowed those feelings to sink into her heart and body. "It was lovely and felt very real, very present," she says. At the same time, she started "conversing with" the mystery man she wanted to bring into her life. "I talked to him as if he already existed—and in reality he did. I just hadn't met him yet," she says. "I believe I was already connected with him before we met. I call it love *before* first sight."

She reminds me of a story my father used to tell about working with Maharashi Mahesh Yogi. At a meeting with Maharashi, a TM member had presented a great idea for a new project, and everyone was excited about the possibilities. Then someone asked, "Where will the money come from?" Maharashi replied: "From wherever it is right now."

"That's where I believed my soul mate would come from," Ford says.

It was my father who told Ford about Amma, the hugging guru. Ford felt that perhaps Amma could provide that "little cosmic power boost" to bring her soul mate into her life. So she signed up for a weekend course during which she would have the opportunity to receive hugs from Amma. When Amma was hugging her, Ford whispered her intent to the guru: "Dear Amma, please heal my heart of anything that is stopping me from finding my soul mate." The next evening, when she received her second hug, she asked Amma to "send me my soul mate." She also mentioned some of the qualities she believed her man would possess.

Three weeks later, Ford had to travel to Portland, Oregon, to meet with a client. When she called his office, his business associate, Brian, told her he would pick her up at the airport. When she saw Brian, a fit, tall, attractive man who seemed to radiate positive energy, something stirred in Ford's soul. Later, as she and Brian worked together that day, Ford heard an internal voice say, *He's the one.*

"Our colleagues who were with us that day noticed what was happening between Brian and me," she says. "It was real and palpable and intense." Before the day was over, Brian confessed that he felt he already knew Ford because he'd seen her in his dreams. And she told him that she recognized him on some level too.

They were engaged within two weeks, and Brian moved to San Diego so they could be together. Exactly one year to the day after Ford asked Amma to help her find her soul mate, Amma officiated at the couple's Hindu marriage ceremony in front of thousands of people. "That was sixteen years ago, and I believe as strongly as ever that we were meant to be together," says Ford, adding, "but I wouldn't have found Brian if I hadn't expressed what I wanted. If you don't ask, you don't get. You have to share your desire with at least one other person to really put it out there, to take a stand for it—to say, 'This is what I desire.' This is what I am creating for my life. Expressing is a way of taking responsibility for what you want."

On New Year's Day, I heed Ford's advice about taking responsibility for what I want and post this on Intent.com: *My intent is to begin 2014 with gratitude, love, inspiration, and hope.* More than anything else, I want this journey to be about learning to live with those ideals, and I believe that every step I take in that direction will be both an expression of my intent and another step toward living with intent.

> "If you don't ask, you don't get. You have to share your desire with at least one other person to really put it out there, to take a stand for it—to say, 'This is what I desire.'"

As the days pass, I try to carry those values forward in my daily life. I continue writing in my gratitude journal, but I also redouble my efforts to express gratitude to the people I encounter throughout the day, both those who are dear to me and those I don't know. One day I'm having a particularly thankful day. I remember to thank the girls for getting ready for school quickly; I thank Sumant for the eggs at breakfast; I pop in and thank the girls' teachers, telling them how grateful I am for their efforts this year. I thank the checker and bagger at the grocery store, the barista who gives me my tea. And I try to make the phrase count. I look in people's eyes and mean the words as I say them. As the day progresses, a feeling builds in my heart that I can only describe as joy. Expressing gratitude makes me feel connected to the whole of mankind, in all our messy, eclectic uniqueness.

Last fall I picked up Brené Brown's book *The Gifts of Imperfection*. The title was appealing for obvious reasons, and Brown had created quite a buzz in the spirituality and self-help circles. Everyone was taken with her research on shame and vulnerability, and even though I've never thought of myself as being overly burdened by shame, I believed I'd benefit from reading her work. Even so, every time I reached for a new book, I passed over hers. But one night not long after my Day of Thanks, as I'd come to think of it, I pick it up, mostly, to be honest, because it's a slim volume—it didn't look quite as overwhelming as some of my other books.

I scan the table of contents, as I always do before plunging in, and my eyes snag one chapter in particular: "Cultivating Gratitude and Joy." Brown's research has given her the opportunity to interview thousands of people across the country, and here's what she says in this chapter: "Without exception, every person I interviewed who described living a joyful life or who described themselves as joyful, actively practiced gratitude and attributed their joyfulness to their gratitude practice." Given my experience, that's not hard to believe.

As the days spin out from under me, like a treadmill that's set a bit too high for my fitness level, I try to continue practicing gratitude, and without fail I get that same warm, glowy feeling in my chest. I also try to express love, which is harder. I'm used to telling my girls I love them, but I'm less verbally affectionate with my friends. I am reticent about being emotional with my friends, but I also see an opportunity to open up a deeper connection with people I care about. As Marianne Williamson says, "Love is what we are born with. Fear is what we learn. The spiritual journey is the unlearning of fear and prejudices and the acceptance of love back in our hearts."

If I want more love in my life, I need to be more loving. But I can't go around saying "I love you" to everyone. That's just not who I am. Besides, they'd think I was nuts. Again, Brown's book helps. She distinguishes between *professing* love and *practicing* love. I don't need to say the words "I love you" to be loving. Expressing love doesn't have to mean saying it. Showing it is an equally powerful form of expression.

So I look for opportunities to show my love as well as express my fondness in words that feel authentic and true for me.

At yoga one day, I tell a friend, "I love your enthusiasm. I have more fun because you're enjoying it so much." She doesn't look at me strangely. She doesn't seem embarrassed by my comment. She seems genuinely moved and gives me a warm hug. Another day, I'm listening to a friend talk about her difficulties with her teenage son. I haven't experienced any of the things she's going through, and in a certain way it makes me uncomfortable to hear them. It's scary to think about one of my daughters smoking pot or drinking. But then I look in her eyes and see the pain she's in, so I just listen. I hold back the judgment, the fear, the tiny voice that says her problems aren't my problems, and I open up to her experience. As she's sitting there, tears in her eyes, she says, "I'm just scared of what's going to happen." And when I respond by saying, "I know what you mean," I actually do. I may not have gone through her experience, but I've certainly been worried about my children and afraid for their well-being. Her experience, I realize, isn't foreign to me at all. By being present and open, I was able to connect with her story on

> Expressing love, whether through words or action, is ultimately at the heart of living with intention. When we act with loving kindness, we bring joy to ourselves and to those around us, which brings more goodness and light into the world.

an emotional level. In that moment, I believe, my expression of solidarity and understanding was actually a declaration of love.

Expressing love, whether through words or action, is ultimately at the heart of living with intention. When we act with loving kindness, we bring joy to ourselves and to those around us, which brings more goodness and light into the world. So I continue working with my love practice. I add a loving-kindness meditation to my usual routine: I hug my mom and tell her I love her when she comes to watch the girls one day; I call my dad to check in; I cook an elaborate dinner for Sumant and the kids. As I reach out—literally, sometimes—to show my affection, I can feel the walls I had constructed around myself (walls I didn't even know existed) start to dissolve. I feel more vulnerable but more connected, less safe but more seen. This work will take some time, I realize, but it's already worth it. By showing people love, I feel more loved—not just by others but by myself.

As Brown says, "Love isn't something we give or get; it is something we nurture and grow, a connection that can only be cultivated between two people when it exists within each one of them—we can only love others as much as we love ourselves."

When we embrace love for ourselves, it is easier to accept love from others. And the more love we feel, the more love we give. It grows and grows, and in turn affects the world around us. Ultimately, expressing our intents is a way to love ourselves enough to say we deserve happiness, connection, and joy. And when we express our intents, we acknowledge we trust ourselves and those around us. By expressing our love, whether verbally or through our actions, we're also putting more love into the world. And if we all make an effort to do more of that, imagine how much good we can do, not just for ourselves, but for future generations.

INTENTIONAL LIVING:
REFLECTIONS AND PRACTICES

I started Intent.com for people to express their intents, and find connection and support from others. Expressing your intents can be done through words and through action.

1. Write a daily intent in your journal, or post it on Intent.com or on our Intent app. This can be an intent for the day or for the week, or you can reaffirm the same intent daily.
2. Today tell one person who is important to you that you love him or her.
3. Practice love through your actions for the day. Hug a loved one, call an old friend, thank the cashier at the grocery store, or smile at the garage attendant.

INTENT PRACTICE: DRAW A MIND MAP

Sometimes expressing your intents is not easy. Drawing a mind map is one way to tap into free-flow thoughts and start to express your deepest desires.

- In the journal section of this book (see page 237) or in the center of a blank piece of paper, write the following question:
  - *What makes me happy?*
- List the things as they immediately come to your mind. Don't feel you need to think too much about your answers. Just write the feelings, actions, emotions, names of people and places, putting those words on the paper.
- Spend one minute or less writing down these words.
- Circle the big ideas on your paper.
- Take a moment and reflect on the big themes you see there.
- For today, choose one of those themes and think about how you can enrich this aspect of your life. Create and write a simple intent around this theme.
- At this point, just writing the intent and planting

the seed is enough. For the next week, state the intent in the morning or before you go to bed. You may find the ritual of saying it at the end of a meditation to be helpful, or post it on Intent.com and reaffirm it every day this week.

- Keep your mind map in a special place where you can refer to it regularly.

Here is a copy of my mind map, and some related intents.

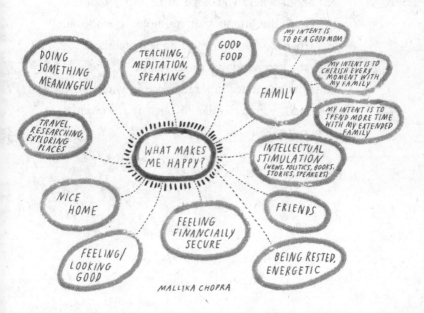

INTENT PRACTICE: WRITE A
LETTER TO YOURSELF

- Choose a beautiful piece of stationery and your favorite pen or marker.
- Take five minutes to meditate and think about your intents for the next six months.
- Date your letter.
- Now write a free-flowing, honest letter to yourself about where you hope to be in six months. What are the intents that you hope to work on, and what are the things you hope to achieve?
- Sign the letter and seal the envelope.
- Now put the letter in a safe place in your house and mark your calendar to open it six months from today.

CHAPTER SIX

NURTURE

I board the plane; stash my book, magazines, and iPad in the seat pocket; take off my shoes; then get my blanket and pillow positioned for the long flight ahead. It's strange to be this relaxed before flying to India. Normally on a long day of travel with the children, I'm completely harried by the time I get this far. Between feeding the kids, downloading shows on their iPads, and making sure they have enough activities for the more-than-twenty-hour trip to Delhi, it's always a sprint. Not today. For the first time in a long while, I'm taking the long flight solo—and quite frankly I feel a little bit as if I just walked into a spa. I've downloaded the first three seasons of *Downton Abbey,* and I'll get to watch them with *no interruptions.* I'm even going to have a glass of champagne with dinner. Living *large,* Mallika style.

I'm heading to India for a week to stay with my mom's

parents, whom we call Nani and Nana. They have been care-takers for their three daughters, six grandchildren, six great-grandchildren, and other extended family their whole lives. Now that they're eighty-nine and ninety-two, respectively, it's our turn to support them. They're still healthy and inde-pendent for their age, but all of us feel more secure when someone is with them. This week my aunt and uncle, who live with Nani and Nana, are traveling in Thailand. My mom recently returned from a visit with her parents, and her younger sister, Geeta, plans to go in a month. They needed someone to fill in, and I decided to do it. It's been far too long—nearly twenty years—since I've stayed in their home, and I love the idea of having them all to myself. Besides, I know their time with us is limited, and I don't want to miss the opportunity to enjoy their company.

Years earlier, after my dad's father, Daddy, died, everyone in our family took turns staying with Maa, my grandmother. It helped her—and the rest of us—get through that diffi-cult time. Now that my girls are older, I feel comfortable joining the rotation with Nani and Nana, especially because my mom is staying with Sumant and the kids while I am away. Still, I recognize how much I've changed in the past months. When I went on the fitness retreat months ago, I was almost paralyzed with anxiety at the idea of leaving my family for a week. Now I'm relishing the opportunity. Could it be that I'm learning to loosen my grip on the parenting reins, one white-knuckled finger at a time?

As the plane surges into the air, I'm flooded by memories of my childhood visits to India with my grandparents. During our annual visits to India, Nani's house was the gathering place for all the aunts, uncles, cousins, friends, friends' cousins, and any stragglers anyone felt like bringing along. Amid the constant stream of visitors, we'd drink endless cups of tea and chew over the latest family conflict or political crisis, while Nani baked brownies and cookies in the kitchen. To this day, the smell of baked goods transports me to my grandparents' home. Nana would take us on picnics to the Gateway of India or for rides on the pedal boats near the Delhi Zoo. Even during my kids' visits just a few years ago, Nani baked constantly while Nana played cricket with the girls in the driveway. No wonder I have such a fondness for India: my perceptions were shaped in large part by the welcoming warmth of my grandparents' home.

My flight lands in Delhi at ten p.m., and when I emerge from customs I find my in-laws waiting. I'm so grateful for the family I married into. I married Sumant when I was twenty-five, so I've essentially grown up with him and his family, and I feel as connected to them as to my own. In the car, I give everyone an update on Tara and Leela and get the scoop on the latest family dramas. We drive to Defense Colony, where my grandparents live, to find my grandmother, clad in her bathrobe, pacing out front. Her white hair gleams in the moonlight. The sight of her takes me back to my teenage years, when my cousin and I would go out at night. No matter how late we got home, my grandmother was always waiting up. I leap from the car and wrap my arms around her ever-shrinking frame, breathing in the familiar scent of Oil of Olay, her favorite cream. "Nani!" I croak, too choked up to say anything more.

My father-in-law carries my suitcase into the house, as my mother-in-law gently scolds my grandmother for staying up. I thank them for the ride, then follow Nani inside. As she gets me settled in the guest room, which hasn't changed in the last thirty years, my grandfather scuttles in, wearing the white kurta he always sleeps in, a shawl draped around his shoulders. He hugs me, but I can tell he's tired, and I beg them both to go to bed. It will take them several days to recover from this late night, but I know there's no way I could have talked them out of it—and their love for me makes me tear up again.

I crawl into the twin-size bed, the mattress as thin and hard as I remember it. Nani has thoughtfully placed a hand-blocked printed quilt at the bottom of the bed, just in case the air-conditioning is too cold. The smell of the sheets and the quilt are familiar and reassuring. I watch the ceiling fan spin overhead, just as I have so many times before. I open up my journal and write:

Here I am in Delhi. It seems like yesterday that I was here, unmarried, being cared for by my grandparents. They were close to my age now when they used to travel to the United

States to care for Gotham and me. How the wheels of time turn!

In the first hour I've been here, my grandparents have checked on me three times to make sure I'm settled and comfortable. I forgot how lovely it feels to be so fussed over and tended. I feel safe, cared for, nurtured.

I awaken with the pen still in my hand, and the smell of tea and biscuits wafting into the room. My grandfather and I sit outside to eat; we hear the local vegetable and fruit vendors call from their wooden carts on the streets. I feel a little jet-lagged, so I head to the park for a quick walk; I'm younger than everyone by a good thirty years, and I can see that the elders are trying to figure out who I am. At some point, word spreads. "That's Rita's daughter," I hear them saying to each other, nodding with recognition. I feel safe, at home, despite being in the midst of strangers. When I return to the house, I take a bucket bath—literally, using a cup to pour water from a bucket on my body, the traditional Indian way of conserving water—then eat Nani's breakfast, accompanied as always by slices of orange and apple, which she insists I eat before leaving the table.

For the next seven days I sleep more than I have in years, eat three healthy meals a day, take walks, catch up with family and friends. But mostly I hang out with my grandparents. It's amazing how quickly I adapt to the slower pace. Adjusting the fans, opening and closing the curtains, preparing meals, enjoying the sound of Nana laughing with someone on the phone, reading the paper, going to the market, visiting with family. In their world, these things are Activities, with a capital A, and I believe there's something to that.

In fact, life suddenly seems so clear to me. As you get older, you winnow your life down to the things that matter the most: Spending time with loved ones. Finding solace in simple rituals. Nurturing your body and soul.

> As you get older, you winnow your life down to the things that matter the most: Spending time with loved ones. Finding solace in simple rituals. Nurturing your body and soul.

Those are the places where happiness lives. I need to remember that. I'm guessing most of us do. It's so easy to let the days slip by in a stream of distracted busyness, but we all need to find ways to somehow stitch simple pleasure into our busy days.

While chatting with Nani and Nana at breakfast one day, it occurs to me that while my personal dramas feel uniquely urgent, in truth they're far less daunting than much of what my grandparents endured. Those two have witnessed everything I could imagine and more. In their twenties they fled turmoil in Pakistan to start fresh as displaced refugees in India; my grandfather served in the air force in World War II; they took a ship through the Suez Canal; they lived in

Europe. I think about the woes Sumant and I have. Paying our taxes and debts, educating our girls, staying healthy, keeping up with work, traveling—it's all been done before, over and over again, since time began, and I actually find that idea wonderfully comforting. We're not alone; we're part of the fabric of human experience—even if not as extreme as my grandparents' version.

As my departure date draws near, one thought keeps running through my mind: *I wish I could pack up Nani and Nana's love and nurturing and carry both back in my suitcase. I wish I always felt this cared-for and cherished, this relaxed and loved.* The irony of that thought isn't lost on me. My intention in traveling halfway around the world was to take care of my grandparents, but the truth is they've actually cared for me. Fed me, entertained me, loved me, nurtured me. Reminded me of what's important. Healed me.

Months ago, when I was making my list of words that described the intent process, "nurture" was one of the first I jotted down. For one thing, it is important to nurture your intents as you move toward bringing them to fruition. Arielle Ford spent months nurturing her vision of finding a soul mate. Andrew Weil's vision to open a restaurant that married the concepts of health food with delicious food took years. His first True Food restaurant opened when he was sixty-six, and in the introduction to his cookbook of the same name, he says, "It's never too late to realize a dream. . . .

If you've nurtured an idea for a long time, I assure you that the decades you've spent incubating it will prove to be a blessing."

"It's never too late to realize a dream. . . . If you've nurtured an idea for a long time, I assure you that the decades you've spent incubating it will prove to be a blessing."

Because intents often don't happen overnight, it's critical to nurture yourself along the way—to be kind to yourself, to accept setbacks as part of the process, to give yourself the breaks you need, and to allow other people to come to your aid when you need a helping hand. My visit with my grandparents provides me with just the emotional sustenance I need to forge ahead.

I've been gone only a week, and yet when I walk through the door of our Santa Monica home, it feels as if it's been months—and reentry is a little bumpier than I would have liked. I'm overjoyed to see Sumant and the girls and intensely grateful to my mom for taking such good care of them. And I'm eager to catch up on their lives. Even so, when they start sharing the details of things that happened at school and at work in my absence, I can feel my blood pressure start to rise. I try to stay calm, present, and supportive. But it's not easy. The chaos, the noise, the demands—and even their stories—are stressing me out!

Later, while lying in bed, I try to figure out why I felt so instantly tense, and I realize their stories triggered that all-too-familiar toxic cocktail of guilt and worry. When Tara told me about the decisions her classmates were making about middle school, I didn't just hear the words, I dredged up all the emotional baggage I attach to them: *Where will Tara go? Will it be the right choice for her?* When Sumant mentioned he'd run into a snag while pulling a major deal together, my mind veered off a cliff, imagining what would happen if the deal fell through.

I close my eyes to meditate, and as I breathe, I remind myself that I need to have faith that things will turn out OK. Instead of flying off into fretting mode at the slightest provocation, I need to stay right where I am—which is to say, the present moment. In the moment, the only thing that's real is what *is*. And tonight what *is* is: I can't sleep.

It's late, but I can't sleep, so after meditating to calm my mind, I pick up Marianne Williamson's *The Gift of Change*. She's a longtime friend of my father's, and although I've always been intrigued by her work, I've never read much of it. Flipping through it, I start scanning a section about stress. "Every time we think, 'Oh, my God, I have so much to do and I don't know how I can do it,' we can change our thinking. We can place all our burdens in the hands of God, ask for a miracle, and thank Him in advance for providing it.... When I remember God's power is unlimited, I stop stressing about how limited mine is."

Oh, brother, I think. *What good is that? God can't drive the kids to school. God can't tell my staff how to handle a crisis or bring in new investors or help me write this book.*

True, says a quieter, less snarky voice. *But by trusting the universe to nurture your intentions, you can release some of the stress. You can choose to let go of your obsessive worrying and have faith that things will work out.*

Despite my resistance, I keep reading. Williamson's point of view reminds me of something I saw on the Chopra Center's website not long ago, so I pull out my laptop, and after a few wrong turns find an article called "10 Ways to Nurture Your Spiritual Life." Number 9 is this:

> *Allow Spirit to lead. . . . Don't listen to the voice that says you have to be in charge, that constant vigilance is the only way to get anything done. Instead, let Spirit try a new way. Intend for everything to work out as it should, then let go and allow opportunities to come your way.*

Could it be that my grandparents' nurturing has been available to me all along, that it exists in the universe or the divine or God or the spirit that connects us all, and I've been too distracted by my own self-importance and overscheduled day planner to notice? Just as important, is there a way to access that feeling of being nurtured, to bring it forward in my life so I don't have to travel halfway around the world to feel it?

In Williamson's book, she says, "Stress is simply the inevitable consequence of thinking the unreal is real. In this sense, stress is a choice." That hits home. Maybe it's not that my life is so complicated. Maybe I'm complicating my life. True, I have more on my plate than Nani and Nana, but I spin the busyness into chaos by worrying about the future and rehashing the past. Could it be that my concern about my life being unbalanced is actually a self-created myth—one I perpetuate by overdramatizing the bad things and under-appreciating the good?

I can't will away my anxiety, nor can I eliminate stressors from my life, but I can learn to put them in perspective, to recognize when I'm getting carried away and to let go of the fantasy that I'm actually in control. The truth is, life will happen whether I worry or not. I know this. So why fight it? Why not slow down, cut everyone some slack, and trust that I will get the support I need?

> The truth is, life will happen whether I worry or not.

As I settle in at home, I try to home in on what it was about being at my grandparents' house that felt so nurturing. One day it occurs to me: I gave myself permission to dawdle. I spent a couple of hours doing a crossword puzzle. I read a really good book. I went to the salon and got my hair washed and blow dried. Granted, I can't while away hour after hour as a working mom, but I can allow myself to do things I enjoy, whether it's going for a walk with a friend or playing hooky and going to see a movie with Sumant during the day. For months I've been chastising myself for wasting time with video games or Facebook. But those things are relaxing, and they give me pleasure. If they don't take time away from my other priorities (like sleep), what's the harm? Maybe the guilt I've been heaping on myself is more the problem than the activities themselves. What if I tell myself instead that it's OK to do things I enjoy, even if they're meaningless? What if I accept that I need to waste time as much as I need healthy food and exercise? What if I welcome activities into my life just because they're fun and feel good? Just thinking about indulging in my "bad habits" free of guilt makes me feel lighter and less stressed—more as I felt in Delhi.

I think of Maa, my father's mother, who sang her morning prayers on the harmonium. My grandmother did not have the greatest singing voice, but she loved learning the harmonium with her friend Ms. Chatterjee, who would visit every few days. Together they would say prayers, gossip, share the latest community news and scandals. Maa was one of the most nurturing women I've ever met, and yet she also took time to nurture herself—to meditate, to pray, to go to the market and buy healthy vegetables, to connect with friends, have fun and do things (even things she wasn't so good at) simply because they gave her pleasure.

What a contrast to my life and those of most women I know! We could learn a thing or two from our elders. I think about a story a friend of mine shared not long ago. A consultant at a strategy firm, she had spent a month working on four major projects simultaneously, and they all had to be delivered on the same date. At the same time, she was caring for her two teenage sons—coordinating sports schedules, driving them to activities, making sure they did their homework, and dealing with adolescent mood swings. On top of that, she was providing emotional support to her husband, who was transitioning from one job to another. Forget about exercising, eating well, sleeping, or taking a break for herself. She was on call 24/7.

One week before her presentations were due, she came down with a terrible case of flu. She was completely knocked out. She couldn't do anything but lay in bed and barely had the energy to go to the bathroom. At the height of her illness, she received an e-mail from her boss asking how she was progressing on her presentations. Instead of being angry, she was flooded by feelings of guilt and failure. She felt she was letting everyone down: her boss, her kids, her husband. Now she was as miserable emotionally as she was physically. But because she didn't feel up to doing anything, she had time to think. And after a week of rest and soul-searching, she realized her sense of duty was out of whack. Yes, she wanted to be a reliable employee, a nurturing parent, and a supportive wife, but she also needed to take care of herself. When she reviewed the priorities in her life, she realized she didn't even make the list. "It sounds trite, but I was reminded of the thing they always tell you on planes—to put on your own oxygen mask before helping others," she says. "I was trying to help everyone else with no oxygen mask at all!"

The first thing she did once she was back on her feet was start a meditation practice. She downloaded a meditation app on her phone and also signed up for the Oprah & Deepak's 21-Day Meditation Experience. She began each day with a short meditation, which allowed her to face her responsibilities with a feeling of control and calm. After a while she learned that by taking short breathing breaks in the middle of the day she could regain a sense of perspective and peace, even when things around her were frantic. "Turns out, that flu was a blessing," she says. "It changed my life."

I think about her now and realize her story is my story—and every woman's. We nurture everyone else at the expense of taking care of ourselves. And while we benefit from giving to others—tending our flock is so deeply satisfying, it must surely be woven into our DNA—we won't feel fully whole until we allow ourselves the same privilege. We must open ourselves to love, accept help, seek support, and trust that there are forces beyond our control that can provide guidance, comfort, grounding, and safe passage. My friend's flu may have been a fluke; then again, it may have been the universe giving her just the break she needed.

If asking for help plays a role in expressing your intent, it's absolutely central to the idea of nurturing it. That lesson hit home a number of years ago when I was pregnant with Tara. I was so looking forward to motherhood, but I also realized that my passion to pursue my professional path was as alive as ever. I had a short window before our baby was born. Why not set the intent to complete my MBA while I still had a little time? Sure, there were logistical challenges. I was four months pregnant and living in Los Angeles, whereas my program was in Chicago, at Northwestern's Kellogg School of Management. But I called the school's dean, Dipak Jain, and he was willing to be flexible in helping me complete my degree. He crafted a program that allowed me to take courses as a visiting student at the Anderson School of Management at UCLA, do independent studies during the weeks after I had my baby, and then return to Chicago to complete the program at Kellogg.

I was incredibly grateful for his support, but there was one big sticking point: in order to carry out this plan, I'd need to be in Chicago with a three-month-old baby. Sumant had a promising new job in LA, so he wouldn't be able to return to Chicago with me. What was I going to do?

I considered abandoning my intent and giving up the dream of earning my MBA, but I knew there was an alternative that might work. The trouble is, it would require asking for help. I hemmed and hawed for a week or two. I didn't want to inconvenience anyone or expect them to put their lives on hold for mine. But I wanted this badly, and there was simply no way I could do it without support, so I finally worked up the nerve to broach the subject. The women guardians in my life—my mom, my mother-in-law, and Meena Masi, my mom's sister who lived in India—didn't hesitate. They said they'd do whatever it took to help me realize my intent to complete my MBA. So after Tara was born, I returned to Chicago, baby in tow, accompanied by my mothers, who rotated taking care of my newborn (and me) while I finished school. I'd breast-feed, dash to class, study, and dash home to the temporary apartment I had rented near campus to feed Tara again.

It was crazy and chaotic—and one of the most magical times in my life. While I was tending my newborn, I was being nurtured by an older generation of women, all of whom supported my ambition. I was reminded of the timeworn phrase "It takes a village." It does. I've tried to create a village on Intent.com and with my mom friends in my community, and I've seen how effective it can be. When people support one another, it creates momentum, instills confidence, and inspires action to take the necessary steps to change. We all need a village. So why is it so hard to ask the villagers for help?

My village includes not only my family but also many of my friends. Romi, who dragged me to the fitness spa, has pushed me in other ways as well. For years, I told her I loved to teach meditation, but I felt I didn't have the time to do it while my kids were young. Finally, one year she'd heard enough. Her kids' middle school fund-raiser was coming up, and she put my meditation services up for auction without even asking me. To my surprise, the item sold out in less than two minutes. And that first meditation class opened the door for many more. By now, my intent to teach meditation has bloomed into a glorious, gratifying reality. I've shared the gift of meditation with thousands of people—but it might not have happened if it hadn't been for Romi's support and faith.

Similarly, I wouldn't be doing yoga today if it weren't for my friends who encouraged me to join them. And without their motivation, I wouldn't make it to those weekly sessions. I've also started going for regular walks with my friend Lara, a great way to catch up and get healthy. My fitness friends inspire me, encourage me, and spur me on—a phenomenon that's been validated by research. Not only are people who exercise with friends more likely to do it regularly, but they're also more apt to push themselves harder during their sessions. We humans are social creatures. We need each other. And when we help each other, remarkable things can happen.

The same concept applies to happiness. It's contagious. Gallup has spearheaded studies that show that if you have one happy friend, you are 15 percent more likely to be happy. Even more interesting, if a friend of a friend is happy, you are 10 percent more likely to be happy. It's the trickle-down theory of joy. Similar correlations are found with weight loss. Friends who band together to lose weight are more likely to be successful than those who go it alone.

And, of course, intents work the same way. By staying connected to my village, I'm nurturing my intents.

It sounds simple, but it's one of the many lessons I've had to learn over and over again. Maybe I'm a slow learner, but I prefer to think otherwise. Instead, I think that perhaps women are programmed by society to go it alone and never admit we need help. (And let's admit it, perhaps men too!) It's an unhealthy message—one we'd be better off getting rid of for good. Almost every impressive thing I've accomplished in my life has required the support of others.

> Almost every impressive thing I've accomplished in my life has required the support of others.

This book is a good example. After I got the idea to write it, the work stalled in the proposal stage. I had trouble moving forward and figuring out what I wanted to say. When I

shared my difficulty with my agent and friend Linda Loewenthal, she said, "Let me help you!" Linda took the various drafts of my proposal and helped me shape them into
a more focused, polished, comprehensive pitch. She pushed
me to write more and poured hours of her own time into
reworking and rethinking certain sections. With her support, I finally had a presentable proposal, one that received
numerous offers when we shopped it around to publishers.

Once I landed a book contract, it suddenly occurred
to me that I'd committed to something huge. I'd need to
research, write, and deliver a book—one that lived up to the
promise of the proposal. I told Linda I was intimidated by
the prospect of tackling such a big project, and she suggested
that I hire someone to work with me. My first reaction came
straight from my ego: *Helloooo, I am the writer here! Why
would I hire someone to help me?* But I thought about it for a
while, and after a few days I grudgingly admitted I would
need help. I agreed to interview a few people, and in my first
conversation, I realized that Linda was right. It was a great
idea to work with someone who knew what she was doing.
Not only that, my whole mind-set shifted. I recognized that
asking for help did not make me less of a writer. In fact, if
I truly wanted to honor my intent to write the best book
possible, asking for help wasn't just the smart thing to do, it
was the *right* thing to do.

Now, months into the project, I couldn't be happier.
Working with my collaborator, Ginny Graves, has been

lively and rewarding and has turned out to be the best deci-
sion I could have made. We brainstorm, talk through chap-
ters, rework stories, share insights, and cheer each other on.
Having a partner has made the project more manageable,
less terrifying—and way more fun.

Even with Ginny's help, and the invaluable support of
Linda and my friends and family, my confidence about
writing a book has vacillated wildly, from periods of feeling
self-assured to more enduring ones during which I question
my sanity. *Why would anyone want to read what I have to say?
What made me think I could do this? I'm such an idiot for committing to something so big!*

On and on march the foot soldiers of my inner critic.
Feeling grateful for the good things in my life, including
the opportunity to write a book, can interrupt their forward
progress, as can confessing my fears to sympathetic villagers. But at the end of the day, those soldiers are still in my
head, hunkered down in well-fortified bunkers, armed with
wounding ammo. I mention this confidence-killing army to
Ginny, and she says she thinks of the self-critical voices in
her head as the Mean Girls. Several days later a book arrives
in the mail. It's called *Self-Compassion*, and it's written by
Kristin Neff, a professor who has researched the topic for

more than a decade. *This book helps me deal with the Mean Girls,* Ginny's note says. *It's time we put those catty bitches in their place!*

I laugh out loud, grateful not only to have the chance to see the humor of my predicament but also to know I'm not alone—and after reading a little of Neff's book, I see that recognizing we're not alone, and taking comfort in our shared, flawed humanness, is a fundamental component of self-compassion.

"The emotion of compassion springs from the recognition that the human experience is imperfect," Neff writes. "Self-compassion honors the fact that all human beings are fallible, that wrong choices and feelings of regret are inevitable, no matter how high and mighty one is. . . . Whereas self-pity says 'poor me,' self-compassion remembers that everyone suffers, and it offers comfort because everyone is human."

When I'm stuck in that self-defeating place, I get so myopic I can't see that everyone else has similar moments. It doesn't help when I go on Facebook and read about all my friends' successes. Facebook is a forum I love for its ability to connect people but also loathe for its relentless focus on the positive. Nowhere among friends' posts do I see their pain, their insecurity, their self-flagellation, and that makes me feel very alone. I've learned that while Facebook is fantastic for getting updates on family and friends' lives, it's not the best place to turn when I'm truly needing connection and support. For that I need my flesh-and-blood loved ones, who can sympathize, commiserate, and through their own stories of struggle, give me the kind of solace and perspective I need to get through the tough times.

As the Beatles sing, "I am he as you are he as you are me / And we are all together." If I can remind myself of that, I won't take my suffering so seriously. If I can tap into the humanity in my insecurity, I'll treat myself with more understanding and compassion. To move from *I'm alone* to *I'm human,* Neff advocates treating oneself like a cherished friend. We need to allow ourselves to be moved by our own pain, she says, to stop, recognize, and acknowledge our own difficult emotions by saying something like, "This is really hard right now." Self-kindness helps us soothe our troubled minds. By befriending ourselves, she says, "[w]e make a peace offering of warmth, gentleness and sympathy *from* ourselves *to* ourselves."

Around the time I'm immersed in Neff's book, I open my e-mail inbox to find a note from Arianna Huffington. I had sent her a note three months before, telling her about my book and soliciting some stories from her about her own experience with failure. When I didn't hear anything back after a week or so, the Mean Girls launched a full-scale assault. *She probably thinks your idea is stupid. Why would you think she has the time to deal with your questions? If she answers, it's probably only because she likes and respects your dad.*

Her kind and honest response reminds me that we all face challenges and setbacks. In her note, she tells me that her second book was initially rejected by every publisher she showed it to, and when she launched the *Huffington Post,* it was widely criticized. As she says in her e-mail, "Huff-post launched to decidedly mixed reviews (including one that said the site was 'the movie equivalent of *Gigli, Ishtar* and *Heaven's Gate* rolled into one') and my second book was rejected by 36 publishers, which amounted to one of the low points of my life. By about rejection 25, you would have thought I might have said, 'Hey, you know, there's something wrong here. Maybe I should be looking at a different career.'"

Instead of throwing in the towel, Huffington reminded herself of a phrase her mother said to her over and over as a child: *Failure is not the opposite of success. Failure is a stepping stone to success.* Still, she was out of money and depressed. "I was walking down St. James Street in London, where I was living at the time, and saw a Barclays Bank. I walked in and, armed with nothing but a lot of chutzpah, I asked to speak to the manager and asked him for a loan. Even though I didn't have any assets, the banker—whose name was Ian

Bell—gave me a loan. It changed my life, because it meant I could keep things together for another 13 rejections—and finally, an acceptance."

Talk about the power of nurturing an intent! Huffington didn't let her self-doubt dissuade her from doing what she needed to do: reach out for help. As she says, "In fairytales there are helpful animals that come out of nowhere to help the hero or heroine through a dark and difficult time, often helping them find a way out of the forest. Well, in life too, there are helpful animals disguised as human beings—as bank managers like Ian Bell, to whom I still send a Christmas card every year. So, very often, the difference between success and failure is perseverance. It's how long we can keep going until success happens. It's getting up one more time than we fall down. Knowing this has been the best motivation."

Her words hit home. The goal isn't to avoid falling. Everyone falls. The goal is to get up, dust myself off, and start over. With the help of nurturing friends—including my own compassionate voice—I feel certain I can create a life that looks more like the one I envision, one that's filled with purpose, meaning, and love.

When I decided to write this book, and explore what it means to truly live with intent, I wrote a long list of people I wanted to interview—and one name was on it from the beginning: Marianne Williamson. She and my father have been friends for more than twenty years. Their writing careers boomed around the same time, and together they helped shape the New Age conversation of the nineties. I've heard her speak and have always been struck by her intelligence. She's strong, unapologetic, and staunchly committed to spreading the gospel of love. When she announced not long ago that she was running for Congress, I wasn't surprised. She's a woman of action who has the power to bring about change, and I was delighted when she agreed to take time out of her busy campaign schedule to speak with me.

Williamson invites me to meet her at her brand-new apartment in West LA. I arrive early and sit in my car reviewing the sections I've highlighted in her books. I want to be as prepared as possible to face this formidable woman. As I head up to her apartment, I wipe my sweaty palms on my pants. The Mean Girls have a heyday with that one. So before I knock on her door, I close my eyes and wrap my arms around myself—another technique Neff suggests for invoking self-compassion. I hold myself for ten or fifteen seconds—and by the time I let go, I feel more composed.

A campaign volunteer meets me at the door. Posters with "Marianne for Congress" lean against a nearby wall, and boxes labeled "DISHES" sit unopened on the kitchen counter. As I sit in the living room, I can hear volunteers in the next room working the phones, soliciting support for Williamson's campaign. It's all quite exciting.

After a few minutes she walks into the room and wraps me in a warm hug. As we begin to talk, I mention the support my mother has given my dad throughout his career—support that allowed him to travel without worrying about whether we kids were well cared for at home—and Williamson laughs. "Tell me about it!" she says. "I didn't have it quite so easy. I had to make rules for my speaking because my daughter always came first. There is no more important work than being a good mother, and that was always my priority. When she was little, my daughter said to me, 'Mommy, I can deal with you being gone for two days, but not for more than that. OK?' And I kept that promise to her whenever possible."

As a single mother, Williamson endured challenges that were far greater than mine, and yet her focus isn't on her own difficulties but on those who face circumstances far more challenging. As she says,

> *Child raising is a job that requires more than one person. I was very aware as a single mother how fortunate I was that my career gave me the resources to hire real help. And I think often about families struggling to meet the demands of both work and parenting. You and I find it a struggle. You and I find it exhausting. But our exhaustion and struggle are small compared with the exhaustion and struggle of many*

other people, particularly those who don't have economic resources. There is a lot of lament that more mothers do not stay home with their children, but that lament is hypocritical given the fact that the average American family can no longer live on a single salary. In our current economic landscape many families can't make ends meet unless both parents work full-time. The accumulated stress this produces is untenable, not just personally for the millions of people who are in this boat, but economically and socially. We need a strong social support system to help people get by.

Nurturing, she adds, is essential for everyone—rich and poor alike. She says she couldn't have accomplished what she has without the godparents and others who made sure her daughter felt a web of unconditional love and support. And she wouldn't be running for Congress without the help and time of many, many people.

As a candidate, I'm relying not only on the support of people who know me well but on the kindness of strangers—and it makes all the difference in the world. We've become too casual in this society with the phrase "I support you." The words are often meaningless—like saying, "How are you?" and not paying attention to the response. But when people say "I support you" and mean, "I will do what I can to help," that's a whole different thing. It's hard to be there for each other today because everyone is under so much stress. But because of that, when people really show up, it means that much more.

Williamson's comments reaffirm for me that we can't go it alone. I wouldn't be able to write this book, teach meditation classes, or give speeches around the country without the support of Sumant, my mom, and the myriad friends who step in to help. It's the people in our lives—the flawed, fallible, wonderful humans—who make us stronger, and it is OK to depend on them and ask for help. Whether it is asking for connections to find a job, getting two kids to two different activities on a Saturday morning, or managing a work project, we get through life thanks to our family, our friends, our neighbors, our village. Our intents survive—and thrive—thanks not only to our own ability to persevere but to our willingness to call on the people around us to help—and their generous, selfless, sometimes miraculous willingness to show up.

> Our intents survive—and thrive—thanks not only to our own ability to persevere but to our willingness to call on the people around us to help—and their generous, selfless, sometimes miraculous willingness to show up.

INTENTIONAL LIVING:
REFLECTIONS AND PRACTICES

"Nurture" means to care for or encourage the development of someone or something. Nurturing ourselves and self-care is as important as nurturing our loved ones or our ideas.

1. Call an old friend or family member whom you haven't spoken to in a long time. Reconnect, even if you are embarrassed that it has been too long.

2. Think about a task you have been avoiding because you don't have time. Ask someone to help you do it.

3. If you had a day at home or in your neighborhood when you could focus solely on your own emotional, physical, and spiritual well-being, what would you do? What would make you laugh, feel joyful? Write down these ideas and set the intent to make them happen. Think about the people who can join you or can support you to make that day happen.

INTENT PRACTICE: THE
SANCTITY OF SUPPORT

Plan twenty minutes—perhaps during a walk, after yoga or meditation, or even when sitting quietly in your home with a cup of tea.

- Think about people in your life who could use your support: loved ones, your child's teacher, someone at work. Note that person (you can do this mentally or write it in a journal).
- Think of ways you can support that person in the next week, perhaps by having a conversation, making an introduction, gifting a spa treatment, or just letting him or her know you care.
- Over the next week act on your intent to support this person. Record your feelings as you embark on this journey.
- Having done that, and experienced what it means to give support, plan another twenty minutes to do the same kind of reflection about who can support you in your intents.

INTENT PRACTICE: MIRROR EXERCISE

Be patient with this exercise—at first it may feel silly and awkward—but it has tremendous power to help you see the positive in yourself. (I still feel uncomfortable at times when I do this. Don't let that stop you!)

- Find a mirror in your home that you can use in private. It could be a mirror in your bathroom or a hand mirror you hold while sitting in bed or a comfortable chair.

- Look at your face in the mirror. Look deeply into your eyes, at the contours of your face, your forehead, the fall of your hair, the color of your lips.

- Notice any initial judgment you may have, and set the intent to let go of self-criticism.

- While looking at yourself, say "I love you." Add your name at the end of the sentence for more emphasis. Spend at least one minute, repeating the words "I love you" every fifteen to twenty seconds.

- Continue looking at yourself, and compliment yourself for something you feel proud of or have accomplished for the day or the week. For example, you might say, "I am proud that I took the time to exercise today." Or "I love that you strive to be a good mother every day." Give yourself five to ten compliments.

- Now to finish the exercise, close your eyes, and take a deep breath. As you inhale, bring loving and healing energy into your body.
- Mentally repeat the words "I *am*," accepting the totality of who you are today.
- Open your eyes.
- Try to repeat this exercise every day for one week

CHAPTER SEVEN

TAKE ACTION

At 7:30 one evening the phone rings. Sumant answers, a smile lighting up his face. "Rajiv!" he whoops, delighted to hear from his dear friend from college. I'm doing the dishes and the girls are busy with homework, so I'm only half paying attention, but within seconds I can tell something isn't right. There's no bantering, no more exclamations. Worse, Sumant's tone has shifted from upbeat to sober. When I turn to look at him, his expression makes my heart skip a beat. The color has completely drained from his face.

"Have they done a biopsy?" he asks. I stare at him, holding my breath, the dishrag in my hands dripping water on the floor. In answer to my questioning look, Sumant scribbles, *Seema has a lump.*

That's not possible.

Just a few weeks before, we'd met Rajiv and Seema for

dinner while they were visiting LA. We laughed, traded stories, reminisced. Seema seemed radiantly healthy, as always. When we went home that night, I said to Sumant, "Seema is one of my favorite people in this world. I'm so glad she's married to Rajiv. We're blessed to have them in our lives."

Now I stand at the sink, dumbfounded, a single urgent phrase chasing itself through my mind: *Please don't let it be serious. Please don't let it be serious. Please don't let it be serious.*

When Sumant hangs up, he slumps into a chair. In a voice tight with emotion, he explains that Seema found a lump in her breast, and a mammogram revealed a worrisome-looking mass. Now they're trying to schedule a biopsy and other imaging tests to determine whether she actually has cancer, but she's having trouble getting in to see anyone quickly. I fly into action, eager to help. I call my father to see if he can connect her with a doctor, and he promises to make some calls.

When I put the phone down, I turn and see Tara staring at us, eyes round with concern. "What's going on?" she asks quietly. She has already heard me use the word "cancer," and although she doesn't understand much about the illness, she knows this: it's scary and it can be serious. My cousin Rishi lost his vision and hearing while he was being treated for a brain tumor, and less than two years ago we all suffered through the heartbreak of the illness and death of my dad's colleague David Simon.

I call the girls into the living room, gathering Leela onto

my lap and holding Tara's hand. "We don't know for certain what's going on," I say, "but Seema found a lump and has to have some tests to make sure it's nothing serious."

Clearly thinking about my cousin, Leela asks, "Will she go blind? Will she die?"

"I have faith she'll be fine," I say, sounding more confident than I feel. "Cancer treatments are very good these days, and Seema is healthy and strong. But we should all send her positive, healing thoughts." The girls look noticeably lighter; sending healing thoughts is the kind of mission they can grasp, and taking action gives them something to focus on other than their fear.

I put the girls to bed and sit in the room with them until they fall asleep, not because they need me there but because it soothes me to be with them. When I come downstairs, Sumant is watching TV, though I can tell he's only half paying attention. I ask about Seema, about how Rajiv is holding up, about what we can do to help. Eventually the conversation veers to other friends who've had cancer. We remind ourselves of the positive stories—the ones in which women have survived breast cancer and gone on to live long, healthy lives. Then I voice the concern that is in the back of both of our minds. "If this happened to one of us, how would we handle it? We're completely unprepared."

Every year we talk about writing our wills to make sure our kids will be taken care of if something happens to one or both of us. And every year, we put it off. Like fixing the drippy faucet in the guest bathroom or cleaning out the garage, it's something we tell ourselves we'll get to someday. Just not today. Or tomorrow. Worse, neither of us has seen a doctor in some time, partly because we can ask my dad for advice, partly because we suffer from the same magical thinking everyone else does: illness happens to other people, not me. My last checkup was four years ago. Before that, I hadn't seen a doctor since Leela was born. She's almost ten. Sumant isn't any better. He's been to a doctor exactly once in the last eight years.

As wake-up calls go, Seema's diagnosis is the absolute worst sort. I'm sick with worry for her and Rajiv. But her diagnosis shakes me out of my complacence and spurs me into action. The next morning, after I drop the girls at school, I call my doctor's office. I'm embarrassed when they try to pull up our records. They have no idea we updated our health insurance three years ago. Next, I call the dentist and make appointments for Sumant and me. I take the girls regularly, but we haven't had cleanings in more than two years—"too long," the receptionist informs me primly, adding, "Everyone needs a teeth cleaning at least once a year." Duly shamed, I write our appointments on the calendar, then dial our investment adviser and tell him Sumant and I are finally ready to draw up the wills we've been promising to do for the last decade. Energized by my actions, I text my friend Holly, who is a personal trainer. *Just checking your schedule. Any chance I could get an appointment sometime soon?*

With that text, the absurdity of the situation hits me. I set the intent months ago to embrace wellness. But until now it had never occurred to me to see a doctor or a dentist, or even to ask Holly for help. I'd thought a lot about what it means to be healthy—I'd envisioned myself training for a half marathon, going gluten free, banishing sugar from my diet—and somehow allowed those fantasies to stand in for many of the practical, concrete steps I needed to take to care of my health. In being so head and heart focused, I'd disregarded some of the less sexy but super important fundamentals of wellness. *If you want to take care of your health, you need to see a doctor. Duh. And I'm a doctor's daughter.*

I believe in the power of expressing intents, but I also know that without action they're often empty words. Every once in a while an intent seems to manifest almost magically, like a gift from the universe. Most of the time, though, we need to pay attention and look for opportunities to bring our intents to life. Intention needs attention *and* active engagement. If you want to take responsibility for your life, you need to take action.

Taking action means doing whatever you can to see your intents come to life, whether it's making medical appointments to care for your health, creating a new résumé to land your dream job, signing up for volunteer work at a homeless shelter, or cutting back to part-time work, if you can, to spend more time with your kids. In the intent process, this is the rubber-hits-the-road step that can catapult you from thinking and talking to doing—and once you're doing, you're on your way to fully living with intent.

I call and text Seema for updates, and within a couple of weeks she gets the news we've been dreading: the lump is cancerous. It's still in a fairly early stage, and her prognosis is good, but she's facing chemotherapy, surgery, and radiation. She has a long haul ahead. She's already started taking steps to ensure that she's as healthy as possible going into the treatment. She's eating well and walking regularly. But the stress is getting to her, so one day I offer to teach her to meditate. I fly to her home in San Francisco, where we spend one fantastic day together—bonding, talking, laughing, crying, and meditating. It's the best gift I can think of to give her—one that fulfills my goal of living with love—and she receives it with such gratitude that it fills me with joy.

I also do what I can to enlist the power of the universe to help rid Seema's body of cancer. I visualize Seema's immune system as a fierce warrior, rallying itself to defeat the deadly invader. I surround her with white light during my own meditation and include the loving-kindness phrases at the end of each sitting, naming all those I love in turn. *May Sumant be well. May Tara and Leela be well. May Seema and Rajiv be well.* My efforts are my non-Christian version of intercessory prayer; the studies show it sometimes helps, and I'm sure it can't hurt. Also, it just makes me feel better.

At the same time, I make an effort to accept the reality that life is scary and unpredictable, that each moment is all we have—and I try to use the urgency of that message to further fuel my motivation not only to be healthier but also to live the kind of life I want to live now, in the present, rather than putting it off for some imagined future.

I need to take action now. We all do. I believe that each one of us was put on this earth to fulfill our own destiny, but it won't magically manifest without concerted effort. We all have things we know we need to do, things we can do today, to bring more happiness, health, and purpose into our lives. The time to start is now.

Thinking along those lines reminds me of a story I've heard in a number of different inspirational talks. It goes something like this:

A man of faith found his village beset by a great storm. He didn't worry about surviving, though, because he knew that God would take care of him. As the waters rose, his neighbors came to tell him that he should leave while he could. He thanked them but said that God would take care of him. The waters rose even more, and the ground floor of his house flooded. A man in a boat paddled up to his bedroom window, and pleaded with the faithful man to escape. *No thank you,* he said. *God will save me.* The floodwaters continued to rise, and eventually the man had to climb to the roof of his house for safety. A helicopter flew overhead, but the man refused to be airlifted out. *God will take care of me,* he told himself. Eventually, the water rose so high that he was swept from his roof and drowned. When he found himself before God, he cried, "I was a man of faith and you abandoned me!" God laughed. "No, you refused my help. I sent neighbors, a boat, and even a helicopter. What else could I do?"

In other words, miracles usually come in the form of everyday opportunities. It's up to us all to seize them. What's holding you back from taking action in your own life? What miracles are in front of you that you're not seeing? What is God or the universe sending your way that you're passing up?

> "Do not ask the Lord to guide your footsteps if you are not willing to move your feet."

As if to hammer home the point, later that day I see this quote on Facebook: *Do not ask the Lord to guide your footsteps if you are not willing to move your feet.*

OK. My feet are moving.

After Seema's cancer diagnosis, I begin reflecting on where I am on my journey of intentional living and what I need to do to move along the process. Have I made changes that are leading to more happiness, healthier living, more balance and inner peace? Absolutely. Emotionally I'm in a much better place than last year. I'm sleeping better than I have in several years, and I'm meditating regularly, which helps not only to keep me calm but also provides daily insight into the way I think and the issues and events that trigger unpleasant emotions. I know myself better now—and I like what I see.

I've reduced my caffeine and sugar intake, although the latter is still an ongoing struggle. I can't pass a bakery without feeling the urge to swing in and grab something—and some days I still do. I've tried to replace baked goods with a piece or two of dark chocolate a day—which according to a *lot* of research is actually a *healthy* choice. It works much of the time—and on the days I indulge in something less virtuous I try to do so mindfully, so I can get as much pleasure from the experience as possible. If I'm going to eat a cupcake, I might as well enjoy it.

When it comes to diet, I've learned an important lesson: I'm not perfect—and I don't have to be. Life isn't perfect, and no matter how hard I try, it never will be. The road to intentional living is paved with bumps, potholes, flat tires, and detours; perfection isn't a stop on that road. Yet there are also stretches of smooth sailing—

> The road to intentional living is paved with bumps, potholes, flat tires, and detours; perfection isn't a stop on that road.

and so long as I'm on the road, I'm heading in the right direction.

One area that I feel less satisfied with is exercise. Despite doing yoga and going for walks with friends whenever I can, I'm still not exercising frequently or intensely enough, and when I tune in to my body during meditation I hear it sending me an urgent move-more message. I feel restless, stiff, unfit, heavy—and that causes ongoing frustration and disappointment.

Because I'm committed to taking action, I once again text Holly, who'd never gotten back to me. She apologizes for being out of touch; she, too, is writing a book and suggests we meet at a trailhead later that day for a hike, then go to the gym to do some beginner strength training. I've never loved working out in a gym, but I text back OK before I can talk myself out of it.

Two hours later she and I are hiking up a steep trail. I haven't done anything this strenuous since the fitness retreat with Romi, and it feels both exhilarating and challenging. An hour later, sweaty and dusty, we head to the gym and work our way through a series of strength-training moves. I don't love the atmosphere. There are too many women with perfect (sometimes perfectly augmented) bodies, and the whole scene feels a little superficial. But taking action on behalf of my body feels good, and I leave the gym energized instead of exhausted. When Pharrell Williams's song "Happy" comes on the radio as I'm driving home, I can't help singing and bopping along. "Clap along if you know what happiness is to you . . ."

Later, my muscles pleasantly fatigued, I tally progress toward my goals and realize that overall I've made net gains. That's great news. But my failures nag at me because they exist in areas that mean a lot to me. I don't feel as if I've made strides in serving my community or enhancing my interpersonal relationships, both of which are high-priority items.

I look back over some of the notes I've jotted down over the past months and reaffirm themes from my mind map that I believe will lead to a more joyful life. I still believe in each one. But how can I fully bring the concepts to life? I'm staring at the paper when I have a thought: I could link two of the themes together and see if that sparks ideas for activities. The approach is similar to something I've seen my dad do at executive-training workshops, and it seems to help people think in more creative ways about their lives. So I randomly draw lines between different concepts in my notes:

I connect Family and Doing Something Meaningful, and Friends and Teaching Meditation. It's amazing how connecting the two ideas creates synergy and sparks ideas. It's a fun exercise, and once the ideas start percolating, I see all sorts of possibilities for how to bring these important themes into my life in more concrete ways. By pairing Family with Doing Something Meaningful, I come up with the idea to volunteer at a food kitchen with my girls. By linking Friends with Teaching Meditation, I realize I could host group meditations for friends. A line between Travel and Good Food helps me come up with the idea of taking a food-themed trip to New York City. (Sumant will like that one.) One way to connect Friends with Intellectual Stimulation would be to start a book club. Excited, I e-mail Romi and Cara to see if they're interested in joining me in a book group next fall. (I already know the end of the year is going to be too busy, and summer will be filled with travel.)

And over time some wonderful things begin to unfold.

Like Sumant, Tara loves to cook, and she and Leela have created a version of the TV show *Sweet Genius*, in which Leela gives Tara a theme and a mandatory ingredient for a dessert. Tara has sixty minutes to prepare the dish and present it to the family. Leela created a PowerPoint outlining the judging criteria, including categories such as execution, creativity, and taste. Of course she almost always gives her big sister perfect 10s. And Tara loves the challenge.

I tell Romi about Tara's love of baking, and it turns out that Romi's daughter, Maddy, has started a project called Take the Cake, in which she and a friend bake birthday cakes every month for kids in a local transitional village, a place where moms (and sometimes dads) and kids live after fleeing an abusive situation or living on the street. The community helps them find permanent housing and jobs and get back on their feet. Maddy bakes personalized cakes for the kids' birthdays—a lovely way to honor the families and help these children in difficult circumstances feel special and recognized.

The opportunity is tailor-made for Tara and me. Yet again, I marvel at the way the universe provides opportunities when you need them. I ask Tara if she'd like to participate, and she's all over it. So I call Romi and tell her we'd love to bake several cakes for the next delivery. Tara invites a friend over one Sunday morning, and together we whip up four cakes: two chocolate with chocolate frosting, one vanilla with blue frosting, and one vanilla with rainbow frosting and sparkles. When we deliver our creations to the village, the rainbow cake goes to a darling pigtailed four-year-old girl in a shiny-pink Hello Kitty T-shirt. Her eyes light up when she sees it, and she runs to Tara and wraps her in a huge hug. The look on Tara's face will be etched in my memory forever. She radiates joy.

Not long afterward I'm driving to pick up the girls from school when I see a placard in someone's yard endorsing Marianne Williamson for Congress. The sign makes me think about what Williamson had said to me about support: *A lot of people say "I support you" and it means absolutely nothing*. In other words, talk is nice; actions are better. I believe in Williamson as a candidate and would like to see her be successful in her bid for Congress. Why don't I do something meaningful to support her campaign?

The next day, I call her and offer to host a meet-and-greet at my house so my friends can get to know her and what she stands for. She accepts enthusiastically. But the second the words are out of my mouth, I feel a surge of worry. I've never hosted an event like this before, and I honestly don't have the slightest idea how to go about it. Besides, I'm already fairly stressed with meeting my book deadline. What was I thinking?

And then I pause. *It's not rocket science. It's just a party.* I call my sister-in-law, Candice. She's great at this sort of thing, and she helps me not only to break down the event into manageable to-dos, she actually offers to cohost it. In the it-takes-a-village philosophy, Candice is mayor of my village. Always game, always supportive, always reliable, always there. I thank her profusely and send a small prayer of gratitude to the universe. Where would I be without people like Candice in my life?

She and I have a healthy network of mommy friends at our children's school, so we decide to talk to our circle first, and sure enough, many of them jump at the chance to hear Williamson speak in such an intimate setting. Women are a critical voting block, possibly more so for Williamson than other candidates, because her message comes straight from

the heart. I'd love it if we could make a meaningful difference in her campaign.

We plan a morning tea so our friends can come to my
house after dropping their kids at school, and the event
is wonderful. Marianne shares her intent behind running
for Congress—namely, that people with money are wield-
ing far too much influence and, as a result, are eroding the
democratic process. Our friends have the chance to ask her
questions, and they're engaged, interested, and enthusiastic.
Marianne has clearly won over some voters. I feel great!

In this moment I also realize the power of taking just
one step, even if it seems insignificant. Every step reaffirms
your intent, then empowers and helps create more energy
for living the life you want. Anytime you act on behalf of
someone else, or yourself, you feel good. What one step can
you take today to move more toward your intent?

An opportunity that presented itself earlier this year keeps
paying dividends. It's an interesting lesson in how intents,
especially when they dovetail with other people's dreams,
often take on a life of their own.

Early in the school year, the principal at Tara and Leela's
school recruited a group of parents to brainstorm ways in
which we could teach our children more about global issues
and the power of resilience. Eager to seize the opportunity,

I came up with the idea of giving each student in Tara's sixth-grade class a copy of *I Believe in Zero*, Caryl Stern's book about UNICEF and preventable childhood illnesses around the world. When I presented the idea to the principal and teachers, they loved it and actually decided to integrate the themes into the spring curriculum to make it more meaningful. I was blown away by their willingness to put in extra time to create powerful learning experiences for the students.

At the same time, another mom at the school, the actress Jennifer Garner, talked to the principal about the work she was doing with Save the Children, another extraordinary organization that helps needy children in the United States and abroad. (One of the realities of sending kids to a private school in LA is that the parents have interesting backgrounds!) Once again, the teachers figured out a way to bring the two opportunities together in the classroom, developing a week-long curriculum that compared child labor in Bangladesh to similar issues here in California.

Since then, the whole experience has evolved into something even broader and more enriching. Tara and two of her friends, who have been invited to become Young Ambassadors for UNICEF, will be visiting the United Nations in New York. They'll learn about issues related to maternal and neonatal tetanus, eat lunch in the Delegate Dining Room, and walk the halls of the UN. At the same time, two other students from Tara's class have been invited by Save the

Children to an annual kids' summit in Washington, D.C., to learn about the plight of American children and what they can do to help, such as lobbying members of Congress around issues that affect children.

When I look at how all these events came together, I see how my intent to do meaningful work (and expose my children to it as well) coalesced with the similar intents of others, and the universe provided numerous opportunities to bring our intents to life. Sometimes the journey isn't exactly what you plan, but by trusting your instincts and doing what you believe you're meant to do, your intent can realize itself in surprising—and surprisingly powerful—ways.

What surprises me most is how gratifying it is to see this intent unfold. It brings me a kind of deep joy few activities do. Study after study has found that volunteering and doing good deeds bring as much, if not more, joy to the giver as the receiver. Researchers say that those who have more social roles believe their lives are filled with more meaning and purpose. In older people, social participation correlates with lower risks of depression, greater life satisfaction, and lower mortality rates. The truth is, when you volunteer your time and services, you probably get more than you give.

My friend and former Intent employee Chelsea Roff echoes these thoughts when we sit down to chat one day. She says that starting her nonprofit, Eat Breathe Thrive, which is dedicated to helping people with eating disorders recover through the use of yoga, helped save her life.

At sixteen she was hospitalized, near death, for severe anorexia. She survived, thanks to the care of the nurses and doctors who nurtured her back to health. And when she was released, she discovered the healing power of yoga.

"My first intent was to nourish my body," she says. "But that was really hard for me to do until I had a way to practice it on the mat. Yoga put me in touch—and keeps me in touch—with what my body needed."

On a hike one day while thinking about all the things she'd been through, an idea that had been incubating for years finally coalesced in her mind: she wanted to start an organization to guide others who had eating disorders through an integrative healing process. Her gratitude toward the people who helped her led her to recognize that service needed to be part of her life.

"I've been the recipient of so much help throughout my life. My therapist gave me almost seven years of free weekly therapy. People had served me over and over again, so when I finally found myself feeling happy and fulfilled and nourished, I knew that it was time to give back." It's the pay-it-forward principle in action.

She raised $45,000 through an Indiegogo campaign, and now that her nonprofit is up and running, it's become more than an act of fulfilling intention. By serving others, she says, she nourishes herself and is more compassionate with herself. "I see my value and self-worth more clearly, and I'm more able to be kind to myself and take care of myself in healthy ways. By doing something valuable for other people, I see my own value more clearly. Giving of myself has made me whole."

Some of the benefits of volunteering come from the social connections it carries with it, and I can see why. When I'm serving food to kids or volunteering at school, I feel as if I'm part of the fabric of humanity. But I also want to connect with friends and loved ones in ways that are purely fun. I can't remember the last time I went to see a movie or had a glass of wine with a friend in the evening. So I sit down one day, scrutinize our family calendar for windows of opportunity, and start scheduling activities I've put off for too long.

I meet a group of girlfriends for cocktails, and we end up having so much fun it turns into dinner. We laugh, we gossip, we talk about books and movies and kids and husbands. How have I missed out on this joyful experience for so long? I wonder as I drive home. There's nothing so emotionally nourishing as an evening with friends.

After that night, more invitations start trickling in. *Do you want to see a movie? There's a great dance performance at UCLA. Do you want to go with me? Wanna meet me for a cup of tea?* I can't accept every one, but the invites pull me further into the current of life. After spending so long in the slower shallows near the shore, it's a fun, exciting place to be.

It's not just my friends I've been neglecting. It's Sumant too. We're homebodies, for sure, but it's important for us to spend time outside as a couple as well. So one night I talk him into trying a new restaurant not far from our house. It's dimly lit and quite romantic, something that Sumant normally squawks at, but he agrees to go. And as I look across the table at my handsome husband, I feel awash in love. I'm worried we'll talk exclusively about the kids, but now that we're out and alone, our conversation ranges from work to politics to vacation plans. We jot down a few ideas, and I can tell he's as happy as I am that we had this time alone.

Another night Sumant and I are invited to attend a fundraising event for the Los Angeles Ballet. We are normally reluctant about attending such events, but because it's linked to a new fund that Sumant is raising for work, we decide it's important to go. By the time we get home from the day's activities, we have about two minutes to get dressed for the black-tie dinner. Worse, when I put on the dress I want to wear, I realize it's too tight; and with few options for such an occasion I'm forced to opt for a loose-fitting Indian ensemble. A bit depressed, I ask Sumant to drop the kids at my brother's house so I can meditate for ten minutes before we leave. I want to get myself centered and ready to socialize.

It doesn't work very well. During my meditation I have trouble getting my mind off the disappointment about my inability to lose weight. I'm proud of my success in other realms, and yet the failure in that one area looms large. I tell myself I need to just start over, that each moment, each day, is an opportunity to make a new choice and find a different way. And yet I feel somewhat helpless. I've tried and failed so many times before.

The letter I wrote to myself at the Ranch sits on my bed-side table. I received it a few months ago, hoping it would shame me into being better about losing weight, but it just sits there mocking me, an indictment of my inability to care for my body. As if to torture myself, I pick up the letter and reread it.

> *Dear Mallika,*
>
> *As I write this letter to myself, I wonder where on my journey I will be. Have I kept my sugar intake to a minimum? Have I committed to a regular fitness program? This week at the Ranch proved to me that I can do it—let go of the sugar and caffeine, eat healthy vegetables, exercise, and push my body to the limit. Remember, Mallika, you can do it if you really want to.*
>
> *I hope, I really hope, that when I read this letter six months from now, I can say that I made the*

adjustments that were right for me. That I haven't
put the weight back on but have lost more. That I feel
healthy and energetic and am moving my body every
day.

   My intent is to continue on this path of wellness,
being healthy for myself and my family. Let's hope I
make myself proud.

                                         From me,
                                         Mallika

Well, I did put all the weight back on. I sit and wonder
if it's too late to make myself proud in this tricky realm. Do
I have what it takes to try again?

When we arrive at the event, I'm taken aback by the
crowd. There are easily three hundred people, and I know
maybe four. We don't typically mingle with the who's who
of Los Angeles, and many of them are here. The fund-raiser
is honoring three well-known women—Lori Milken, Jane
Seymour, and Paula Abdul—for their work, time, and dedication to ballet and dance.

I enjoy the entire evening, but once Abdul takes the
stage, I'm riveted. Behind her petite physique lies an incredible inner strength, and her story carries a message that
seems tailor-made for me in this moment.

Passionate about dance from the time she was young, she
explains that when she heard about auditions for the NBA
cheerleading squad the Laker Girls, she was determined to

try out, even though she didn't fit the stereotype. "No blond hair, no blue eyes, no long legs," she says. Still, she drove to the LA Forum, where thousands of girls with similar aspirations had already gathered.

When it was her turn to audition, she was cut in the first few minutes. "I'd already faced so much adversity that I'd developed the mantra that 'no' is just the beginning of a negotiation," she says. So she headed to a bathroom stall, prayed for another chance, took a new outfit from her bag, changed her hairstyle, got another audition number under a different name, and reauditioned. The judges cut her again. Still undeterred, she made up yet another name, and went back out on the floor. This time, she was chosen for the team. Within a year, she became the Laker Girls' choreographer and was soon working with the most celebrated names in entertainment.

I leave the event feeling inspired. Setbacks don't have to stop you. If you work hard and you're determined to pursue your dreams, anything can happen.

Needing an extra little bit of inspiration, I call Jeff Pulver, an old friend, social media influencer, and founder of Vonage. He is my weight-loss role model. He set the intention to lose one hundred pounds in a year, and posted it on Facebook. He also bought—and read—forty-one books on health, wellness, fitness, and food. "The advice varied widely, but the one thing they all agreed on was that you have to exercise and build muscle to raise your metabolism," he says. So he enlisted the help of a fit friend, and together they started working out. The first day he could manage only five minutes.

He started posting pictures of his workouts and results from his medical exams on Facebook, and the feedback and support he received was overwhelming. "I discovered love," he says. "First, friends started encouraging me, and then other people heard about it, and all of a sudden I had all these strangers urging me on." After six months, he was able to do a ninety-minute workout combining cardio and strength training.

"There's no one-size-fits-all approach to weight loss," he says now. "Everyone's DNA is different. We're all unique. But I can tell you that putting on muscle helps. And the power of the crowd is indescribable. If you can find ways to connect with other people who want to do the same thing, it will help you achieve your goal."

The minute I get home from our conversation, I send a note to friends. *Does anyone want to start a walking group?* I've been walking with one friend, but I believe that a group might take on bigger, tougher adventures. I'm amazed by all the yeses that pour in. It's too hard to find a time that works for everyone, so I book half a dozen walking dates with individual friends. They dot my calendar for the next month, tiny blooms of purpose and pleasure amid the rest of the to-dos.

I also remember some practical tools my dad uses in his workshops. Attributed originally to management consultant Peter Drucker, SMART goals are often used in the business context. SMART is an acronym that different people use in slightly different ways, but one of the original versions resonates with me:

- Specific
- Measurable
- Attainable
- Realistic
- Timely

It sounds like a reasonable approach. I'm not like Jeff. I know I'm not going to lose gobs of weight, nor do I have to. Dramatic isn't my style, but practical is—and this approach strikes me as eminently practical. So I set a specific goal: I want to lose five pounds in the next two months. It's measurable; it's attainable (doctors say a reasonable goal is a pound a week); it's realistic (although I'd love to lose fifteen, that number sounds overwhelming and unmanageable); and it has a time frame.

I don't know whether I'll be able to pull it off, but what I do know is that taking action on so many fronts has been a tonic. Maybe my positive energy will spill over into weight loss. Even if it doesn't, I've reaped so many wonderful rewards: I feel more connected, more fulfilled, more at peace. Losing a few pounds pales in comparison.

Before starting this project, I thought I was too busy to go out with friends or volunteer for any outside activities. But with Seema's diagnosis, I had an epiphany. I don't have time to sit on the sidelines. None of us do. Life is too short to procrastinate.

Taking positive steps toward our goals—moving from thought to action—provides forward movement, even if it is measured in baby steps. It instills confidence and bolsters momentum. Life is filled with uncertainty, but putting one foot in front of the other is a way to take control and seize the day. It just may be the most optimistic action any of us will ever take.

INTENTIONAL LIVING:
REFLECTIONS AND PRACTICES

Taking action on an intent requires attention, but it should also prove to be fun and rewarding. Taking action also requires commitment and energy, but the benefits are incredibly satisfying.

1. Create a SMART goal around one of your intents, a goal that is Specific, Measurable, Attainable, Realistic, and Timely.
2. Imagine how you will feel when you are living with one of your intents realized. Create a scenario, perhaps in your home or office, with any relevant people around you. Don't be shy about imagining specific details and emotions.
3. Identify a friend who may share a similar intent to yours. Talk to him or her and explore pursuing it together.

INTENT PRACTICE: LINKING
DESIRES TO ACTION

- Take out your mind map, and spend a few minutes reviewing the words you put on the map.
- Draw lines between different themes. Do not think about the relationship between the categories—in fact, the more random the connection the better.
- Choose two themes that are connected. Spend a few minutes honoring how each of these desires makes you feel.
- Now, think of things you can do that will bring these two themes alive together.
- Write down five ideas of how you can take action around these linked themes.
- Choose one. Set a goal to achieve this action item.

EIGHT

LIVING WITH INTENT

We wake up at six for the early-morning drive to Riverside, where Leela has a soccer tournament. Last night we cut apples and oranges and packed a bag with granola bars so we'd have snacks throughout the day. Before we leave, Tara and Leela eat a full breakfast—boiled eggs, fruit, toast, and organic chicken hot dogs, Leela's favorite. She has a long day of sports ahead. We've never been to Riverside, which is about seventy miles inland from where we live in Santa Monica, but the soccer season has presented a whole lot of firsts for our family.

When I was a kid, my immigrant parents were completely oblivious to American traditions like Saturday-morning soccer. While my friends were donning shin guards and scoring goals, I was wrapping *ghungroos*—bracelets with bells—around my ankles and learning to perform the graceful, rhythmic moves of Bharatanatyam, classical Indian dance, with my cousin and best friend. We carpooled into the city to join other Indian girls, and I loved it. In many ways I felt very American, but I knew I looked different from some of my friends and that my parents and culture were different too. Studying Bharatanatyam filled the gap and gave me a sense of cultural identity that was critical at that age. It connected me to the deep beauty and spirituality of my ethnic heritage—and the intimate joy of the dance studio suited my shy intellectual temperament far better than a rowdy soccer field.

When Tara was eight, I found a well-known Bharatana-tyam teacher in Los Angeles, and paid for a year of classes, eager to introduce my older daughter to the movement that had brought me so much joy. At first Tara enjoyed the classes, but before long I could see she had lost interest. Her friends were doing other things, and she wanted to join them. I was conflicted. I didn't want to force my experiences on her—I wanted to respect her individuality—but I felt the loss of the tradition keenly. Dance was one of the few ways I had stayed connected with my Indian heritage. Without it, would my kids retain their cultural identity, their sense of Indianness? We were immersed in American culture, activities, and attitudes, and I worried that this vital tradition from our heritage would be lost. I felt protective of our uniqueness and wished I could find some way to preserve it. Perhaps Leela would carry on the tradition, I told myself. Alas, two years later, when I broached the topic with my younger daughter, I could see it was a lost cause. She was interested in three things: computer programming, robotics, and drumming. Indian dance? Not a chance.

So instead of fighting my daughters, I joined them. I signed them up for soccer through the American Youth Soccer Organization. Soon our Saturdays felt very American indeed. We'd get up, go to Tara's game, grab some lunch, and then rush to Leela's game. I was out of my element, as was Sumant. I volunteered for the least amount of work possible—helping organize the kids into groups on photo day—and watched, dumbfounded, at the competitiveness of some parents. *These are eight- and eleven-year-olds,* Sumant and I said to each other over and over again. We stood out like sore thumbs. We were not only one of the few non-white families on the field, we also weren't comfortable with the intense yelling and cheering. I typically took the girls to their games and would stand awkwardly on the sidelines until Sumant arrived with our double macchiatos and morning scones. As soccer moms go, let's just say I am not the poster child.

Perhaps that's why the soccer mom image became emblematic in my mind over the last few years of the many ways in which I'd lost my way as a person. The persona didn't fit, and I felt lost. It was discomfiting to feel as if I were trying to be someone I was not. While I drove the girls to practices after school or handed out cut apples during half-time, I wondered how my education and so-called global sophistication had led to this. *Shouldn't I be out discussing politics, thinking of ways to end hunger, saving the world?*

The reality is that soccer isn't a perfect fit for my family. The girls aren't aggressive or particularly talented players. It's partly our fault because Sumant and I didn't play catch or kick the ball around when they were young, so they've never felt at home on the field. While some parents are disappointed when their kids don't score a goal, Sumant and I just pray our girls won't mess up or get hurt. We're relieved when they kick the ball in the right direction.

Truth is, we don't value athleticism the same way many American parents do; for us, academic performance is the thing that really matters. On the spectrum from soccer mom to tiger mom, I'm way closer to the latter. We support and encourage our girls' forays into soccer for practical reasons: it's good exercise and they can learn valuable lessons from being part of a team.

> On the spectrum from soccer mom to tiger mom, I'm way closer to the latter.

Leela's soccer season started badly. A girl booted the ball, and it flew straight into Leela's face, bloodying her nose. She had recurring nosebleeds for three weeks afterward, and she became, if possible, even *more* tenuous on the field. Fortunately, her dedicated and kind coaches continued to encourage her to overcome her fear, and even though she's the tiniest and least experienced kid on the team, she showed some improvement. And the coaches' skill paid off big time for the team. They ended up winning every game of the season. On the day of the local championship tournament, Leela had a high fever and couldn't play. We were disappointed that she would miss the last game, but Sumant and I were secretly grateful the season was over. We would finally have our Saturdays back!

Later that afternoon we learned the team had won. The coach and his daughter stopped by our house with Leela's medal and championship pin. We were so grateful for his thoughtfulness and dedication. And despite Leela's lack of skill as a player, she took enormous pride in her medal—examining every minute detail carefully. We saw it meant a lot to our daughter that her team had won, regardless of where she stood in the team's pecking order. I had a fleeting thought then. *If Leela could learn to love soccer, why couldn't I? What was I resisting, exactly?*

As I thought about those questions, I realized that part of my struggle with embracing my daughters as soccer players and my own soccer mom status had to do with culture; I cherished my Indian heritage, and the soccer tribe felt foreign to me. Could they ever be my people, with their robust enthusiasm and competitive gusto? And if I bought into that sports culture, was I in some way rejecting my own, more spiritual past? Was I sacrificing my uniqueness?

Her team was headed to the regional tournament, so several weeks later we drove across town to Culver City

High School, and as we parked our car in the school lot, we realized we'd entered a different league. Even I could tell these kids had real skill. Our girls didn't stand a chance. Or so I thought.

Leela's team played three games that day, and in the final nail-biter to determine the tournament winners, our players found their rhythm and scored goal after goal, keeping up with a team we thought we could never beat. After four quarters, we were tied, and each coach sent his five best players in for overtime. In an incredible move, our best player scored and we won! Leela ran out to the field, clearly overjoyed, and celebrated with her teammates. This time, Sumant and I were as swept up in the excitement as the other parents. We cheered, cried, and congratulated the girls. And then we looked at each other and raised our eyebrows. *Ugh, more soccer . . .*

A month later, we're finally driving to Riverside for Leela's divisional championship game. The girls will play three games, and if they win, they'll have another two tomorrow. This is the real deal. We have a dog sitter staying with Yoda, and we've booked a room at the Riverside Mission Inn so we can turn the event into a weekend away. We have no idea what to expect. Our weekend trips are almost always to San Diego or San Francisco; we're urbanites through and through.

What could have been merely out of the ordinary becomes truly extraordinary when we reach Riverside. The town is filled with people dressed in nineteenth-century clothing—women in gowns and bonnets, men in calf-length coats, vests, and top hats. As Sumant checks us into the hotel, the girls and I head to the lobby bathroom, where we have to squeeze by three women in hoop skirts to get to the stalls. The hairstyles, makeup, jewelry, and shoes—every detail of the outfits is impeccable to the time, as is their formal nineteenth-century diction.

Turns out it's Riverside's annual Charles Dickens Festival. There are street fairs, readings, and food festivals—a nice counterpoint to all-soccer-all-the-time. We're amused, bewildered, and delighted in equal measure.

We leave our bags at the hotel and head to the soccer fields, where we're almost as shocked as we were by the nineteenth-century festival. There are at least forty fields laid out side by side, and games are already in progress on each of them. The spectator areas are packed with families who've settled in for the day with beach chairs, beverage coolers, and snacks. The tournament draws people from all over Southern California, and the diversity is amazing.

Sumant and I look at each other and burst out laughing. Would we ever have guessed when we met eighteen years ago that we'd be taking our daughter to an all-day soccer tournament, surrounded by avid parents and people dressed in period costumes? "Surreal" doesn't begin to describe it.

And somewhere inside me a dam bursts. I laugh so hard I double over and tears roll down my cheeks. All the aspirations and expectations I've had for myself feel far away and slightly silly. *This is what matters,* I think. *This is what it's all about. This absurd moment and the joy that comes from being with my family and sharing experiences. This is my meaning.*

I take it all in. The girls' happy faces. The chaos and competitiveness of sports. The playfulness of the Dickens festival. The sliced apples, the skinned knees, the timid efforts and the fierce ones, the high fives and fist bumps. *You're not in Chopraland, Mallika. But it doesn't matter. This is who you are. This is what's important in your life right now. This is what the universe wants from you. Go ahead and do the other things: teach meditation, start companies, spread the word about intent. Those things are important, but they'll have their moment in good time. For now it's time to embrace your inner soccer mom.*

Leela's team plays magnificently. They don't win the tournament, but she is ecstatic about their accomplishment and feels like she is part of something truly special. At the celebratory dinner—at a local bar surrounded by people in corsets and top hats—I see how a simple shift toward acceptance can make all the difference in one's life. The inadequacies and uncertainties and doubts that have plagued me for months seem almost mad in this moment. I'm grateful for my husband and the family we've created, proud of my baby girl for facing her fears, and delighted with Tara, who has been a supportive older sister. In the warm glow of these gifts, my insecurities fade into the background, and I see clearly how ridiculously, crazily blessed I really am.

Accepting our blessings isn't just about seeing the sunny side or looking at the world through rose-colored glasses. It's seeing things as they really are, the light and the dark, and choosing to embrace the light. It's a struggle for all of us to focus on the good things when the bad weigh heavily on our minds. But it's worthwhile to consider whether you're giving as much energy to the good things in your life as you are to the stressful/worrisome/scary—and if you're not, try to shift the balance in favor of appreciation.

> But it's worthwhile to consider whether you're giving as much energy to the good things in your life as you are to the stressful/worrisome/scary—and if you're not, try to shift the balance in favor of appreciation.

The effort pays off. Appreciation is where hope, optimism, and love live.

My Soccer Tournament Epiphany, as I think of it now, didn't come out of the blue. The truth is, my mind-set had been improving for some time. Whether it's my commitment to meditation, noticing my thoughts, trying to shift my internal dialogue, practicing trust, expressing gratitude, getting involved in meaningful activities, sleeping more, eating better, or reminding myself to savor the moment, I've been feeling a whole lot more centered and happy.

And thanks to all the reading and reflecting I've done over the past year, I've been laying the groundwork for a larger insight. Now it's finally come. The wisest thing I can do is celebrate who I am at this stage of my life rather than worry about who I'm going to be once the girls leave home. It's not the revelation I expected, and yet a part of me wonders why I'm surprised. I've always felt that being an engaged, present, loving parent is the most purposeful thing I can possibly do. It's a job filled with meaning, brimming with joy, permeated by hope, and suffused with love. In answer to the question *How can I serve?*, the response doesn't get much better than that.

I had felt a push-pull between being ordinary and extraordinary, between being a frequency holder, as Eckhart Tolle says, and someone who makes a splash. In our extroverted, selfie-crazed culture, there's constant pressure to stand out, to be different, to make a mark, to be seen. But it's OK for all of us to be ordinary and accept what our lives bring us in the moment. That doesn't mean we forget about meaning and purpose or give up on our dreams; it means we embrace the meaning and purpose that already exists in our lives—*right now*—and let our best intents guide each moment as best we can. It means we give up our egos and connect with something larger than ourselves. It means we become who we truly are—even if that person exists quietly outside the limelight.

As these thoughts are swirling in my head, I see more clearly why I've struggled to come to terms with my soccer mom status. It's partly cultural pressure to pull my weight as a modern woman. It's partly intellectual need: I want to use my mind and make good on my education. It's partly ambition. But there's also a hefty dose of family pressure. It's self-imposed, of course. No one is pressuring me to become something great. But I feel the weight of our family history nonetheless. Fulfilling larger-than-life intents is something of a family legacy.

My grandfather, my father's father—Daddy—became a doctor at a time when that goal was almost unattainable in British India. Indians were not allowed to receive medical training. However, my grandfather studied harder than any of the white men around him and was noticed for his knowledge by a British doctor who championed him (and changed the law in his favor), and Daddy eventually traveled to London for his medical education, becoming one of the first Western-trained doctors in India. His natural skill and gentle nature drew people to him. He attracted a loyal following and even became the personal physician to

Lord Mountbatten, the last viceroy of India. He was living his intent to heal. By the time India achieved independence from the British, Daddy was one of its most respected doctors.

At twenty-five he married my grandmother Maa, a woman with grace, intellect, and a strong personality. She, too, came from a family that emphasized education, for daughters as well as sons. She was outspoken and fiercely protective of her loved ones, and she became the matriarch of her extended family and community.

Daddy persuaded my father to become a doctor, but ultimately he realized his true intent was to heal people through words—through his bestselling books and his groundbreaking insights and ideas about the mind and the universe. The choice was right for him. Over the past two decades he has earned worldwide respect and phenomenal acclaim.

As I reflect on my family's past, I see that the bar is set extremely high for my brother and me. The trouble is, I've spent so much time worrying about how to vault over it, I've never stopped to consider whether I even had the desire to jump that high. And now that I *am* considering, I see that the answer is yes and no. I have inherited some of my father's ambition and vision, and I feel drawn to continue his work.

> But my way isn't the highway. It's the quiet country lane, the less traveled back road.

But my way isn't the highway. It's the quiet country lane, the less traveled back road.

The reality is I possess a healthy dose of my mother's reticence and reserve. Like her, I prefer to shine out of the spotlight. But that doesn't mean her light is any less bright. Far from it. She's the power behind the throne. My mother's patience, guidance, and sacrifices have kept our family on track and given me the confidence, voice, and empowerment to explore, dream, and find my own way. I watch her with my girls and marvel at her energy and attention. She plays, laughs, and sings with them. She treats them as individuals who have their own ideas, thoughts, and desires. She talks to them, teaches them about the world, asks them questions. She never feels she has to justify who she is or what she does. She is proud to be a mother and grandmother.

Of all those who came before me, my mother has had the most profound influence in shaping my destiny. She's the most stable force in the lives of our family, and she is driven by the most powerful intent of all: love.

There is a Native American practice that respects family lineage by encouraging you to ask certain questions before speaking or acting. "Will it honor the parents, the parents' parents, and the parents' parents' parents? Will it serve the children, the children's children, and the children's children's children?" I wonder, does my uniquely messy mix of motherhood, entrepreneurship, and meditation teaching live up to the legacy of my past? After reflecting on my life this year, I believe the answer is yes.

We all have a unique mix of gifts, talents, perspectives, so the challenge is finding your own wonderful mix. Doing so is one of the surest ways to help you live with intent, because intents blossom from your soul, from who you truly are. Getting to know yourself isn't always easy, but the effort pays off with greater clarity and a deeper sense of purpose. We don't all have fame in our futures, but that doesn't mean we won't be recognized. Earning the respect of family, friends, and neighbors; creating a reputation as a good human being; sharing our gifts with those we touch—these things are as valuable and worthy of recognition as accomplishments that receive worldwide acclaim.

As I awaken to my purpose, I start to notice those around me who are living with intent quietly and without fanfare: the frequency holders. They bring consciousness to everyday life through their small activities and interactions, Eckhart Tolle says. "In this way, they endow the seemingly insignificant with profound meaning. Their task is to bring spacious stillness into this world by being absolutely present in whatever they do. . . . They affect the world much more deeply than is visible on the surface of their lives."

I don't need to look far to find someone who fits the bill.

One morning at the girls' school, I listen to Dorothy Menzies, the head of school, as she tells the students and parents about a volunteer opportunity, and it strikes me that this woman could be the poster child for living with intent. Dee, as we call her, has been the head of Carlthorp School for more than thirty years. She has overseen the education of thousands of children, and plays an active role in local community organizations as well. She has a reputation as someone who not only provides children with a stellar academic education but also teaches them to be exemplary human beings.

Why didn't I think of interviewing her before? I ask Dee if she's willing to talk to me about living with intent. She says she'd love to participate but adds that she's surprised I'd want to include her and shouldn't feel any pressure if the interview doesn't work out. She's the first person I've approached to say anything so humble, and it makes me admire her even more.

Dee discovered a love of teaching in her early twenties and never looked back. She taught elementary school, high school, college, and found ways to connect with students, no matter what their age or economic background. But a tragedy imbued her teaching—and her life—with an even deeper sense of purpose. Her beloved thirteen-year-old daughter, Allison, died suddenly of a pulmonary embolism. The terrible loss could have derailed Dee's future. But learning to live with the pain—and find meaning in her life in spite of the loss—has defined her life's work ever since.

"You never get over the loss of a child, but you learn how to live with it," she says. "Allison had a huge personality and huge spirit and an incredible sense of humor, and her presence changed my life. One of the ways I honor her memory is by carrying her spirit forward and letting it serve as an inspiration for my daily choices. She may not be here in person, but her presence is very alive, and I strive to be a good example for her every day.

"When things get difficult, as they do for all of us, my mantra is 'With God's help, I can do this.' And then I put one foot in front of the other and take things step by step. It's partly faith and partly discipline. But it's a combination that works."

> "When things get difficult, as they do for all of us, my mantra is 'With God's help, I can do this.' And then I put one foot in front of the other and take things step by step."

Dee isn't flashy or famous, but at my daughters' school, where the children of movie stars, high-powered executives, and striving authors walk the halls, she is the guiding light who shines the way. She creates a structure that is reassuring to young children. She is a patient helper for both children and parents. She guides the students' moral lives, boosts them when they are scared or unsure of themselves, and encourages them to live up to their potential. She is a role model for everyone—teachers, students, and parents alike. In her quiet, reliable way, she lifts us all up and carries us along. She is the embodiment of living with intent.

As thoughts of love, honor, and service spin in my mind, the Indian festival of Holi approaches. Known as the festival of colors—and also the festival of love—Holi celebrates the coming of spring and the triumph of good over evil. During Holi, people throughout India celebrate by throwing and rubbing colored powder on each other—a symbolic celebration of the abundance of spring colors. The festival takes place on the streets, in parks, at temples. It's a free-for-all, made even messier by the addition of water balloons, hoses, and water guns.

I've never seen anything like it in the United States. It's a bacchanalia. There's music, dancing, drumming. Multiple generations, all social classes, friends, and strangers play together. Adding to the delirium, everyone consumes ample alcohol, and many take bhang, a legal form of cannabis that is mixed into a milky beverage. I tried it one year during Holi after I met Sumant and laughed for more than an hour. It was one of the few times I've ever thrown myself into an experience with complete abandon. It made me feel deeply, wholly alive.

When we moved to the United States and had children,

I planned to introduce my girls to the major Indian festivals, such as Diwali, the celebration of the new year, and Holi, but I struggled to figure out how. My friend Supriya made an effort every year to host a small group of our Indian friends at her house to celebrate Diwali. We'd say a traditional *puja*, or prayer, eat, and exchange gifts, as per the custom. I admired Supriya's active effort to create experiences for her children that connected them to their heritage, and I appreciated the fact that she included us in her parties. But when she invited us to Holi parties, I always begged off. I told myself it wouldn't feel authentic, that there was no way to capture the joy and abandon of the festival outside of India, and that sharing it with lots of people we didn't know would just feel awkward and forced. I vowed that at some point I would take the girls to India to see and participate in the experience *for real*.

This year, however, as Holi approached I felt differently. We should embrace this tradition (without the bhang), live in the *now*. I read something in Brené Brown's book that seals the deal. "Laughter, song and dance create emotional and spiritual connection; they remind us of the one thing that truly matters when we are searching for comfort, celebration, inspiration or healing: we are not alone."

I call Supriya, and ask if she'll include us in her Holi celebration. She's delighted we'd like to come and extends the invitation to Tara's and Leela's friends, my brother's family, and anyone else we want to invite. I'm moved by her generosity, and grateful for it as well.

We arrive at the potluck picnic loaded down with kids, pizzas, cupcakes, and water guns. The other moms have made Indian food, and Tara and her friends savor every bite of the samosas, *bhel puri,* and stuffed *parathas.* I hear Tara describing each of the different foods, and in her tone of voice I hear something that makes my heart sing: pride. She's not just happy to be sharing her culture with her American pals, she sees how special it is. Meanwhile, Leela and her best friend, Krishu, Gotham's son, are quietly filling water guns. It's typical of them. They have no idea what lies ahead, but they're not going to be caught unawares when it does.

We're all eating and socializing when out of the blue one of the dads launches a sneak attack, throwing a huge pitcher of colored water on a group of us. We're all soaked—and ready for revenge. "Happy Holi!" he sings out. And chaos ensues.

Everyone scrambles to grab cups of colored powder and douse whoever is within reach. Pink, green, blue, yellow, purple—the colors fly through the air like living rainbows, coating people's hair and clothes. We look like Warhol paintings come to life. I watch as Supriya grabs a handful of pink color, sneaks up behind Sumant, and rubs it into his silver-gray hair. Sumant leaps to his feet and sets off after Supriya at a gallop. Distracted, I narrowly escape an onslaught from Tara and her friends, then turn away, only to find Leela and Krishu in front of me, water guns blaring, giggling maniacally. They soak me, then dash off, one going left, the other going right, a strategy they obviously planned before the attack.

We're all having a ball—kids, parents, grandparents, Indians, non-Indians. It's pure bliss. My throat tightens with emotion as I watch my daughters discover the magic of this Indian ritual. They throw themselves into it with complete abandon. I think of their still-somewhat-timid approach on the soccer field. They're not shy now, dripping wet and covered in color. All my worry about giving them an "authentic" Holi experience was for naught. It's not where you celebrate Holi that matters. It's the joy of the celebration itself—the cathartic release of pure play. Now I know why Holi is known as the festival of love; where people play, laugh, and celebrate together, love thrives.

> It's the joy of the celebration itself—the cathartic release of pure play.

I grab a cup of powder and toss it on Leela, then run as fast as I can in the other direction.

As my deadline nears, I'm hoping I'll find a fairy-tale ending or pot-of-gold moment. Instead, two weeks before the book is due, I wake up with a head that feels as if it's filled with molten lead and a body overrun with aches. My skin hurts, my toes hurt, my eyelashes hurt. Sumant is out of town, so I call my neighbor and friend Leslie to ask her to take the girls to school. Next, I call my mom and beg her to come help for a few days. I stay in bed for the next three days, coughing, wheezing, aching, feverish, and totally miserable.

The days tick by, my deadline drawing ever closer, and I can't even muster the energy to worry. But in my Nyquil-induced haze, I wonder if this is a sign. Is this a message from the universe telling me to think about the big picture? If so, what picture am I supposed to see?

Waiting for some aha moment, I mull over the past year and the events that brought me to where I am now. All my meditating and soul-searching has led to a noticeable shift in my emotional well-being. I've made some changes at work so I have more time at home. As a result, I feel more connected to my family. And although I've embraced the role of soccer mom, I realize it in no way diminishes my intellectual ability or the possibility of future professional accomplishments. I feel more at peace in the moment and hopeful about the future. Despite the fact that I'm lying in bed with a 102-degree fever, I'm happy.

Even six months ago an illness like this would have made me anxious—worried about what was happening without me, guilty for not pulling my weight. I had so bought into the notion that I had to do it all, and do it all well, that even an illness would have felt like a failure. Now I melt into the fever's steamy embrace. Before I drift off, I jot down these words: *It's not about leaning in or opting out. It's about being real in the moment and making choices that are right for me.*

Marianne Williamson says, "Joy is what happens to us when we allow ourselves to recognize how things really are." I think back to Leela's soccer tournament, and the moment when I recognized the joy of being present as a family. The thing that was also there was love. And I see now that it surrounds me every day.

Love is here in my bedroom. It's in the hot water with honey that my mom left on my bedside table. It's in Leslie's car as she drives my girls to school. It's in the food wrapped neatly in foil in the fridge, dropped off by various friends and family over the course of the past couple of days. It's in the chicken soup I had last night for dinner. It's at Intent, where my team texts me to let me know everything is going smoothly. It's in Sumant as he prepares the girls' breakfast and lunch, walks the dog, wipes down the counters, brings me doses of Nyquil. It's in San Francisco with him as he steps in for me on a mommy/daughter Girl Scout weekend. I think about my cool alpha male husband hanging out with Tara's troop and laugh out loud. And when Tara texts me— *We're having so much fun, Mom!*—that love goes straight to my heart and fills my soul.

While Sumant and Tara are in San Francisco, I drag myself out of bed to meet my mom and Leela for lunch. Leela tells us about her favorite scenes from the movie *Rio 2*, which she has just watched with my mom, and I cherish every word. She's laughing, talking animatedly with her hands and her whole body, and her expressions are truly priceless. I've barely spoken to her in three days, and I swear she's grown and changed in seventy-two hours. Tara texts me a photo of a sock market and tells me her troop has bought a bunch of socks to donate to a youth shelter in the city. I feel a surge of pride—a moment my mom shares. I look across the table at my mom and feel grateful for the

> Love is here in my bedroom. It's in the hot water with honey that my mom left on my bedside table. It's in Leslie's car as she drives my girls to school.

billionth time that she loves my daughters as much as I love them. And then it hits me. She feels the same way about me.

Maybe it's my weakened state, but I'm overcome with feeling. I think about an interview I saw with Maya Angelou, who had died just a few days prior, in which she says,

> *I am aware that I am a child of God. It's such an amazing understanding to think that the "it" that made fleas and mountains, rivers and stars, made me, too. What I pray for is humility to know that there is something greater than I.*

When I feel my mother's love, I feel loved, period—by God, the universe, the divine. And it must be the same when I give love to my daughters, my husband, my parents, my friends. Love binds us together and lifts us up.

This year hasn't been about losing ten pounds or giving up sugar or being on an organized schedule or even doing something great in this world. It's been about finding who I am and embracing the real me—the Mallika who is smart, capable, insecure, silly, strong, quiet, vulnerable, and *whole* just as I am—part of the greater whole that connects us all. My job now is to allow that person to be as real and loving and joyful and present as she can be in every moment.

That's what we *all* need to do. To find out who we truly are and let that person's strengths shine through and lead the way toward greater purpose and peace. By tapping into our inner gifts and living each day in alignment with our best, worthiest, most honorable intentions, we'll find our path through the world.

As we finish our dessert (yes, I still eat sugar), Leela lifts her water glass, and in a mock-adult voice says, "To us." My mom and I giggle and lift our glasses as well.

To all of us, I smile.

To living with love, purpose, joy.

To living with intent.

AFTERWORD

by Deepak Chopra

Mallika's story is relatable because it is a journey we all take. Messiness, chaos, confusion, turmoil, even pain and suffering, are part of the journey, and can even make it interesting as long as we don't get stuck there. When Mallika was born, I was not half as sane as she is now, nor was my life in order, orchestrated as it was by addictive patterns and behaviors. Had it not been for their mother, my wife, Rita, our children might have grown up to be troubled adults—as for many years, I set a poor example.

Rita's life purpose has always been to be the total embodiment of motherhood. I now know that motherhood is the most sacred profession there could ever be. What could be greater than being a catalyst for the unfolding of the infinite potential that is present in a child? Now that I am in the autumn of my life, I realize that I transformed my addictive patterns into an obsession for healing. This was a long and turbulent road, but in my opinion, I did find myself slowly transforming into an authentic healer of body and mind.

So what is my purpose now? It might be almost absurd for people to find out that other than deriving immense joy from being in the presence of my grandchildren, my only purpose now is to rest in existence, awareness, and equanimity.

I now feel like a train traveler, getting ready to pack my bags for my final destination. For this final destination, even though my bags are packed, I will have to leave them on the train.

Here are some insights that might be useful for those ready to make use of them.

The ultimate goal of all intention and desire is to have lived a life of fulfillment. The following keys to fulfillment I've gleaned from a lifetime of experience with many trials and tribulations along the way. Here they are:

1. Learn to nurture your body with sleep, movement, and healthy food. And listen to its wisdom, which expresses itself through signals of comfort and discomfort. When choosing a particular behavior, ask your body, "How do you feel about this?" If your body sends a signal of physical or emotional distress, watch out. If your body sends a signal of comfort and eagerness, proceed.

2. Learn to live in the present, for it is the only moment you have. Catch yourself when you're not in the moment. Otherwise, your life will pass by like a waking dream. Keep your attention on what is here and now. Look for the fullness of life in every moment. Accept what comes to you totally and completely so that you can appreciate it, learn from it, and then let it go. The present is as it should be. It reflects the infinite laws of nature that have brought you to this exact thought, this exact physical response. This moment is as it is because the universe is as it is. Don't struggle against the infinite scheme of things; instead be one with it.

3. Take time every day, even if it is for five to ten minutes, to be silent, to reflect, and to meditate. Ask yourself, Who am I? Is there a "me" beyond name and form? Ask this deeper true self of yours what it really wants. Learn to appreciate a quiet mind. Over the years, I have realized that a quiet mind is more powerful than a positive mind. While optimism is good, a contrived mood of positivity can be actually quite stressful and exasperating to others. If you learn to quiet your internal dialogue and pay attention to your inner life, you will be guided by intuition rather than

externally imposed interpretations of what is and isn't good for you.

4. Relinquish your need for external approval (for me, this has been a lifelong struggle). At a certain point, if you are self-aware, you realize that you alone are the judge of your worth, and your goal is to discover infinite worth within yourself, no matter what anyone else thinks. There is great freedom in this realization.

5. When you find yourself reacting with anger or opposition to any person or circumstance, realize that you are only struggling with yourself. Putting up resistance is the response of defenses created by old hurts.

6. Know that the world "out there" reflects your reality "in here." The people you react to more strongly, whether with love or disgust or hate, are projections of your inner world. What you most dislike is what you most deny in yourself. What you most love is what you most wish for in yourself. Use the mirror of relationships to guide your evolution. The goal is self-knowledge. When you achieve it, the thing that you most want will automatically be present, and what you most dislike will disappear.

7. Shed the burden of moral judgment—you will feel much lighter. Judgment imposes right and wrong

on situations that just are. When you judge, you cut off understanding and shut down the process of learning to love. In judging others, you reflect your lack of self-acceptance. Remember that every person you forgive adds to your self-love.

8. Don't contaminate your body with toxins, either through food, drink, or toxic emotions. Your body is more than a life support system. It is the vehicle that will carry you on the journey of your evolution. The health of every cell in your body contributes to your state of well-being, because every cell is a point of awareness within the field of awareness that is you.

9. Replace fear-motivated behavior with love-motivated behavior. Fear is the product of memory, which dwells in the past. Remembering what hurt us before will direct our energies to making certain that an old hurt will not repeat itself. But trying to impose the past in the present will never wipe out the threat of being hurt. That only happens when you find the security in your own being, which is love. Motivated by the truth inside you, you can face any threat because your inner strength is invulnerable to fear.

10. Understand that the physical world is just a mirror of a deeper intelligence. Intelligence is the invisible organized or all matter and energy,

and because a portion of this intelligence resides within you, you share in the organizing power of the cosmos. Because you are inseparable, linked to everything, you cannot afford to foul the planet's air and water. And at a personal level you cannot afford to live with a toxic mind because every thought makes an impression on the whole field of intelligence. Living in balance and purity is the highest good for you and the universe.

I'm sure you have heard bits and pieces of this kind of advice along the way. Some of what I have mentioned may even sound like cliché, but that does not make it less profound or useful. I gradually welcomed these intentions into my life—some without struggle, some with great difficulty, and some through real suffering. If you live intentionally, the day surely comes when addictions to sensation, power, and security start to lose their foothold. Addictions get replaced by attachments. Attachment gives way to preference. Preference is followed by choice and subtle intention and letting go. The highest state, to use a phrase of the great Indian philosopher Jiddu Krishnamurti, is choiceless awareness, in which the right response to every situation comes to you as it happens. This is the state that wisdom traditions call total freedom. All wisdom traditions aspire to it. This is my wish for Mallika, for my grandchildren, and for all of you who read this book.

LIVING WITH INTENT:
A CHEAT SHEET

Incubate:

Quiet your mind to tap into your deepest intentions; see where this leads.

Notice:

Become mindful of your thoughts and actions and pay attention to what they tell you about what gives you meaning and a sense of purpose—and look for signs that can point you toward your true path.

Trust:

Have confidence in your inner knowing—and in the messages the universe sends you—and allow that knowledge to guide you forward.

Express:

Write down your intentions; say them out loud or share them with others to fully embrace them and help you move ahead in your journey.

Nurture:

Be gentle with yourself as you try to find your way. Intention isn't always a straightforward path, just like life, and giving yourself opportunities to try—and fail—is often part of, and even crucial to, the process.

Take Action:

Once you've identified an intent, or even multiple ones, don't sit and wait for it to magically manifest; instead take the practical steps that can make each become a reality. It may be easiest to choose one intent first and set short-term goals to help you get started.

MY INTENTS TODAY

_____

_____

_____

_____

_____

_____

_____

_____

_____

_____

_____

_____

_____

_____

_____

_____

_____

_____

_____

_____

_____

_____

MY INTENTS TODAY

MY INTENTS TODAY

_____
_____
_____
_____
_____
_____
_____
_____
_____
_____
_____
_____
_____
_____
_____
_____
_____
_____
_____
_____
_____
_____
_____

MY INTENTS TODAY

_____

_____

_____

_____

_____

_____

_____

_____

_____

_____

_____

_____

_____

_____

_____

_____

_____

_____

_____

_____

_____

_____

_____

_____

MY INTENTS TODAY

_____

_____

_____

_____

_____

_____

_____

_____

_____

_____

_____

_____

_____

_____

_____

_____

_____

_____

_____

_____

_____

_____

MY INTENTS TODAY

_____
_____
_____
_____
_____
_____
_____
_____
_____
_____
_____
_____
_____
_____
_____
_____
_____
_____
_____
_____
_____
_____
_____

MY INTENTS TODAY

MY INTENTS TODAY

_____
_____
_____
_____
_____
_____
_____
_____
_____
_____
_____
_____
_____
_____
_____
_____
_____
_____
_____
_____
_____
_____
_____
_____
_____

MY INTENTS TODAY

_____
_____
_____
_____
_____
_____
_____
_____
_____
_____
_____
_____
_____
_____
_____
_____
_____
_____
_____
_____
_____
_____
_____
_____

MY INTENTS TODAY

_____

_____

_____

_____

_____

_____

_____

_____

_____

_____

_____

_____

_____

_____

_____

_____

_____

_____

_____

_____

_____

_____

MY INTENTS TODAY

_____

_____

_____

_____

_____

_____

_____

_____

_____

_____

_____

_____

_____

_____

_____

_____

_____

_____

_____

_____

_____

_____

_____

MY INTENTS TODAY

_____

_____

_____

_____

_____

_____

_____

_____

_____

_____

_____

_____

_____

_____

_____

_____

_____

_____

_____

_____

_____

_____

_____

_____

MY INTENTS TODAY

MY INTENTS TODAY

_____
_____
_____
_____
_____
_____
_____
_____
_____
_____
_____
_____
_____
_____
_____
_____
_____
_____
_____
_____
_____
_____
_____

MY INTENTS TODAY

_____

_____

_____

_____

_____

_____

_____

_____

_____

_____

_____

_____

_____

_____

_____

_____

_____

_____

_____

_____

_____

_____

_____

MY INTENTS TODAY

_____
_____
_____
_____
_____
_____
_____
_____
_____
_____
_____
_____
_____
_____
_____
_____
_____
_____
_____
_____
_____
_____
_____

MY INTENTS TODAY

_____

_____

_____

_____

_____

_____

_____

_____

_____

_____

_____

_____

_____

_____

_____

_____

_____

_____

_____

_____

_____

_____

MY INTENTS TODAY

_____

_____

_____

_____

_____

_____

_____

_____

_____

_____

_____

_____

_____

_____

_____

_____

_____

_____

_____

_____

_____

_____

_____

MY INTENTS TODAY

_____
_____
_____
_____
_____
_____
_____
_____
_____
_____
_____
_____
_____
_____
_____
_____
_____
_____
_____
_____
_____
_____
_____
_____
_____

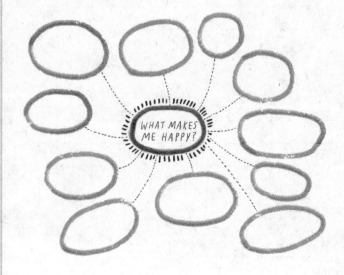

MY BALANCE WHEEL

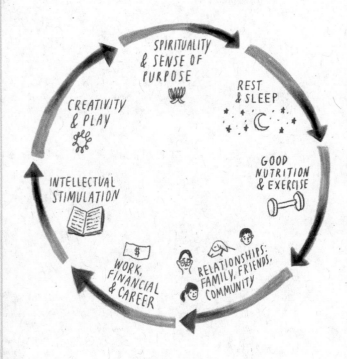

1–3: SUFFERING

4–7: STRUGGLING

8–10: THRIVING

INDEX

ABOUT THE AUTHOR

Mallika Chopra is a mom, media entrepreneur, published author, and a notable voice in the fields of parenting, meditation, and the power of intention. Her previous books, *100 Promises to My Baby* and *100 Questions from My Child*, have been translated and sold in more than twenty countries.

Mallika is the founder of Intent.com—an online destination for turning your intentions into tangible actions, and inspiring others to do the same. Her intent is to harness the power of social media to connect people from around the world to improve their own lives, their communities, and the planet.

Visit Intent.com to read Mallika's blogs, share your own intents, connect with others, and download the free Intent app to incorporate intention into your daily life.